Comparative Human Resource Management

Context is increasingly recognised as a critical explanatory variable in accounting for commonalities and differences in human resource management. Giving expression to it in research models holds the prospect of enhancing theory development, deepening our appreciation of embedded practices in diverse territories, and opening up new lines of enquiry. However, contextualisation presents a significant research challenge and increasingly, international academic research networks that bring together scholars from different countries in the co-production of knowledge represent a key approach to rising to this challenge.

This volume documents aspects of the development of one such network, namely the Cranet Network on International Human Resource Management, and presents a series of recent contributions from the network. The chapters highlight, *inter alia*, the limits to convergence in human resource management as a result of contextual determinism, the role of institutional actors, markets, and work regulation in accounting for variations in practices, the contextual specificities and dynamics at play in transition economies, along with key methodological challenges that arise when seeking to build cumulative comparative knowledge via network collaborations of this nature.

The chapters in this book were originally published as a special issue of *International Studies of Management & Organization*.

Michael J. Morley is Professor of Management at the Kemmy Business School, University of Limerick, Ireland. His research interests encompass international, comparative, and cross-cultural human resource management.

Noreen Heraty is Senior Lecturer and Director of the MSc in Human Resource Management at the Kemmy Business School, University of Limerick, Ireland. Her research interests include international human resource management and development, ageism in the workplace, and psychological contract breach.

Comparative Human Resource Management

Contextual Insights from an International
Research Collaboration

Edited by
Michael J. Morley and Noreen Heraty

LONDON AND NEW YORK

First published 2021
by Routledge
2 Park Square, Milton Park, Abingdon, Oxon OX14 4RN

and by Routledge
605 Third Avenue, New York, NY 10158

Routledge is an imprint of the Taylor & Francis Group, an informa business

Chapters 1 and 3–7 © 2021 Taylor & Francis
Chapter 2 © 2019 Wolfgang Mayrhofer, Paul N. Gooderham and Chris Brewster. Originally published as Open Access.

British Library Cataloguing in Publication Data
A catalogue record for this book is available from the British Library

ISBN: 978-0-367-76769-3 (hbk)
ISBN: 978-0-367-76770-9 (pbk)
ISBN: 978-1-003-16846-1 (ebk)

Typeset in Minion Pro
by Newgen Publishing UK

Publisher's Note
The publisher accepts responsibility for any inconsistencies that may have arisen during the conversion of this book from journal articles to book chapters, namely the inclusion of journal terminology.

Disclaimer
Every effort has been made to contact copyright holders for their permission to reprint material in this book. The publishers would be grateful to hear from any copyright holder who is not here acknowledged and will undertake to rectify any errors or omissions in future editions of this book.

Contents

Citation Information

The chapters in this book were originally published in *International Studies of Management & Organization*, volume 49, issue 4 (2019). When citing this material, please use the original page numbering for each article, as follows:

Chapter 1

The Anatomy of an International Research Collaboration: Building Cumulative Comparative Knowledge in Human Resource Management
Michael J. Morley and Noreen Heraty
International Studies of Management & Organization, volume 49, issue 4 (2019), pp. 341–354

Chapter 2

Context and HRM: Theory, Evidence, and Proposals
Wolfgang Mayrhofer, Paul N. Gooderham and Chris Brewster
International Studies of Management & Organization, volume 49, issue 4 (2019), pp. 355–371

Chapter 3

A Comparative Study of Trade Union Influence over HRM Practices in Spanish and Brazilian Firms: The Role of Industrial Relations Systems and Their Historical Evolution
Wilson Aparecido Costa de Amorim, Andre Luiz Fischer and Jordi Trullen
International Studies of Management & Organization, volume 49, issue 4 (2019), pp. 372–388

Chapter 4

The Antecedents of Comparative Differences in Union Presence and Engagement: Evidence from Coordinated and Liberal Market Contexts
Michael Brookes, Geoffrey Wood and Chris Brewster
International Studies of Management & Organization, volume 49, issue 4 (2019), pp. 389–401

Chapter 5

Understanding Financial Participation across Market Economies
Elaine Farndale, J. Ryan Lamare, Maja Vidović and Amar S. Chauhan
International Studies of Management & Organization, volume 49, issue 4 (2019), pp. 402–421

Chapter 6

Contemporary Human Resource Management Practices in Russia: Flexibility under Uncertainty
Veronika Kabalina, Olga Zelenova and Kira Reshetnikova
International Studies of Management & Organization, volume 49, issue 4 (2019), pp. 422–440

Chapter 7

The Cranet Survey: Improving on a Challenged Research-Practice?
Jesper Christensen, Frans Bévort and Erling Rasmussen
International Studies of Management & Organization, volume 49, issue 4 (2019), pp. 441–464

For any permission-related enquiries please visit:
www.tandfonline.com/page/help/permissions

Notes on Contributors

Frans Bévort, Assistant Professor, Copenhagen Business School, Copenhagen, Denmark.

Chris Brewster, Henley Business School, University of Reading, Reading, UK.

Michael Brookes, Hertfordshire Business School, University of Hertfordshire, Hertfordshire, UK.

Amar S. Chauhan, PhD Candidate, Political Science at Washington University, St. Louis, MO, USA.

Jesper Christensen, PhD Fellow, Copenhagen Business School, Copenhagen, Denmark.

Wilson Aparecido Costa de Amorim, Management Department, FEA USP Faculdade de Economia e Administracao da Universidade, de Sao Paulo, Sao Paulo, Brazil.

Elaine Farndale, Professor, School of Labor and Employment Relations, Pennsylvania State University, University Park, PA, USA; Department of Human Resource Studies, Tilburg University, Tilburg, The Netherlands.

Paul N. Gooderham, Department of Strategy and Management, Norwegian School of Economics, Bergen, Norway.

Noreen Heraty, Senior Lecturer and Director of the MSc program in Human Resource Management, Kemmy Business School, University of Limerick, Limerick, Ireland.

Veronika Kabalina, Professor, Faculty of Business and Management, National Research University Higher School of Economics, Moscow, Russia.

J. Ryan Lamare, Associate Professor, School of Labor and Employment Relations, University of Illinois at Urbana-Champaign, Champaign, IL, USA.

Andre Luiz Fischer, Management Department, FEA USP Faculdade de Economia e Administracao da Universidade, de Sao Paulo, Sao Paulo, Brazil.

Wolfgang Mayrhofer, Interdisciplinary Institute for Management and Organizational Behavior, Vienna University of Economics and Business Administration, Vienna, Austria.

Michael J. Morley, Professor of Management, Kemmy Business School, University of Limerick, Limerick, Ireland.

Erling Rasmussen, Professor, Auckland Technical University, Auckland, New Zealand.

Kira Reshetnikova, Associate Professor, Faculty of Business and Management, National Research University Higher School of Economics, Moscow, Russia.

Jordi Trullen, ESADE Business School, Ramon Llull University, Sant Cugat, Spain.

Maja Vidović, Assistant Teaching Professor, School of Labor and Employment Relations, Pennsylvania State University, University Park, PA, USA.

Geoffrey Wood, DanCap Chair of Innovation and Head of DAN Management, Western University, Canada.

Olga Zelenova, Associate Professor, Faculty of Business and Management, National Research University Higher School of Economics, Moscow, Russia.

Introduction

The Anatomy of an International Research Collaboration: Building Cumulative Comparative Knowledge in Human Resource Management

Michael J. Morley and Noreen Heraty

Abstract: Comparative human resource management (HRM) has an established pedigree in the management and organization literature. However, the generation of novel contextual understanding to enhance theory building, deepen our appreciation of embedded management practices in more diverse territories, and open up new lines of enquiry was, and remains, challenging social science research. Increasingly, international academic research networks that bring together scholars from different countries in the co-production of knowledge represent a key approach to rising to this challenge. In this issue, we document aspects of the development of one such network, namely the *Cranet Network on International Human Resource Management*, and we provide an exposition of a series of recent articles from the network. The contributions highlight, *inter alia*, the limits to convergence in HRM as a result of contextual determinism, the role of institutional actors, markets and work regulation in accounting for variations in people management practices, the contextual specificities and dynamics at play in transition economies, along with key methodological challenges that arise when seeking to build cumulative comparative knowledge via network collaborations of this nature.

INTRODUCTION

The problem for researchers from one culture or context wishing to conduct research on another culture is that the outsiders' past experiences will not have equipped them to make sense of events in the same way that insiders would. (Easterby-Smith and Malina 1999, 84)

Collaboration via international cooperative research networks and the co-production of knowledge are on the rise, as are accounts of their functioning, of their impact on those who participate in them, and of the features and contributions of their scholarly output (Bournois and Chevalier 1998; House et al. 2002; Jonsen et al. 2013; Lowrie and McKnight 2004; Parry, Stavrou-Costea, and Morley 2011; Rigby and Edler 2005; Von Glinow, Drost, and Teagarden 2002). While there are a myriad of reasons underlying this development and significant variations in how it has taken hold across different disciplines, within management and business research it can be read in at least two different ways. Firstly, from a philosophical perspective, it can be viewed as a fundamental effort towards enhancing theory building and deepening our understanding of practices in an era in which the domain of management research has become more international (Geringer, Frayne, and Milliman 2002; Rousseau and Fried 2001). Secondly, from an historical perspective, it may be read as a form of redress in the face of an increasing realization that many contextual features of management practice in numerous territories have not been fully landscaped. The correction of this deficit requires comparative enquiry focused on under-researched regions in order to augment and rebalance the body of knowledge, plug research gaps, and unearth and give expression to indigenous features of management (Leung 2012; Jackson 2013; Tung and Aycan 2008).

Consequently, there is a growing line of thought which broadly supports the argument that valuable insights into organizational systems and preferred approaches will come from studying them in a comparative way. However, comparative enquiry of this nature remains "a challenging undertaking for HRM researchers" (Cooke, Veen, and Wood 2017, 220), often requiring poly-contextually sensitive research approaches designed to unearth "multiple and qualitatively different contexts embedded within one another" (Shapiro, Von Glinow, and Xiao 2007, 129). Despite some of the obvious challenges that are inherent in contextualization, it has been argued that "significant progress has been made in research in the variations in HRM across national boundaries, in both the quantity of studies and theoretical advancements since the mid-1980s" (Cooke et al. 2017, 196). In this effort, academic collaboration and the building of communities of scholars has emerged as a fundamental piece of the architecture necessary for assembling and curating comparative contextual HRM insights (Lazarova, Morley, and Tyson 2008).

This rise in the quantity and the quality of international comparative research on variations in HRM across cultures and territories, the emergence of collaborations in the co-production of new empirical and theoretical insights and the value of cooperative research networks as conduits to delivering such contextual insights, in combination, represent a pertinent point of departure for our purpose in this issue. We bring to readers aspects of the establishment and functioning of the *Cranfield Network on International Human Resource Management* (Cranet) and selected examples of the debates and analyses that form the corpus of research that has emanated from this network of collaborators to date.

BACKGROUND TO THE RESEARCH NETWORK AND DATA COLLECTION

Established in 1989 with five founding member countries (France, Germany, Spain, Sweden, and the UK), Cranet is now comprised of national member universities and business schools from over 46 countries and territories worldwide (Australia; Austria; Belgium; Brazil; Bulgaria; Canada; China; Croatia; Cyprus; Czech Republic; Denmark; Estonia; Finland; France; Germany; Greece; Hungary; Iceland; Indonesia; Ireland; Israel; Italy; Japan; Latvia; Lithuania; Nepal; Netherlands; New Zealand; Norway; Philippines; Portugal; Romania; Russia; Serbia; Slovakia; Slovenia; South Africa; Spain; Sweden; Switzerland; Taiwan; Tunisia; Turkey; Turkish Cypriot Community; UK; USA). These members of the Network collaborate to carry out a regular survey of organizational policies and practices in comparative HRM in each of their respective countries. In this effort, they seek to chart aspects of the landscape of HRM in different socio-cultural contexts and diverse geographic territories (Parry, Stavrou-Costea, and Morley 2011). Cranet is now the largest HRM research network in the world and the only one that has been collecting comparative data on HRM in an array of diverse contexts for three decades.

A common questionnaire, collaboratively designed by Network members, serves as the central data-collection tool. It is developed in English in the first instance, translated into each local language by the National Partners, and then retranslated back into the English language for confirmation purposes. Reflecting on this fundamental aspect of the Network's endeavor, Lazarova et al. (2008, 1998) note that members collaborating in the questionnaire design "have had to establish a common interpretation of the terms so often used unquestioningly by HR academics and practitioners alike; words which may have different meanings in different cultures and languages and which do not translate exactly into English (for example, the word and concept of 'cadre' in French)." The result is that the drafting of the questionnaire and its revision in preparation for a data-gathering round typically requires a combination of sequential meetings and electronic exchanges that can extend over an 18-month period. This is then followed by an extended period of data-collection involving the distribution of the questionnaire to the most senior HR executive in each respondent organization drawn from a representative sample in each participating country. While originally the survey was conducted on a yearly basis, early in the collaboration it became apparent to Network members that policies and practices in the HRM domain were not likely to change with such frequency. In addition, Network members quickly established that a more protracted period for rigorous data analysis was necessary between rounds of data collection. As a result, the Network took a collective decision to extend the time-line between data collection rounds to a three/four year cycle. Table 1 below sets out details of the growth of the Network and the rounds of data collection completed to-date.

ESTABLISHED RESEARCH LEIMOTIFS IN THE NETWORK AND CONTRIBUTIONS TO THIS SPECIAL ISSUE

A total of six articles from Cranet collaborators have been selected for inclusion in this issue. Spanning the theoretical, the empirical, and the methodological, these papers continue and extend the debates and leitmotifs that have been central to the collaboration for three decades, and reflect aspects of the discourse more broadly on continuity, change, and contextualization in management. In particular, the articles offer insights into aspects of four specific lines of enquiry in comparative HRM research, namely, the limits to convergence as

TABLE 1

Member Countries and Communities of Cranet and Participation in Survey Rounds

Country	1989	1990/1991	1992/1993	1995/1996	1999/2000	2004/2005	2008/2009	2014/2015
Germany	•	•	•	•	•	•	•	•
France	•	•	•	•	•	•	•	•
Spain	•	•	•	•	•	•	•	•
Sweden	•	•	•	•	•	•	•	•
United Kingdom	•	•	•	•	•	•	•	•
Denmark		•	•	•	•	•	•	•
Italy		•		•	•	•		•
Netherlands		•	•	•	•	•	•	•
Norway		•	•	•	•	•	•	•
Switzerland		•		•	•	•	•	•
Finland			•	•	•	•	•	•
Ireland			•	•	•		•	
Portugal			•	•	•			
Turkey			•	•	•	•		•
Austria			•		•	•	•	•
Czech Republic			•		•	•	•	
Greece			•		•	•	•	•
Belgium					•	•	•	•
Australia					•	•	•	•
Bulgaria					•	•	•	
Japan					•		•	
Cyprus					•	•	•	•
Israel					•	•	•	•
Tunisia					•	•		
Hungary						•	•	•
New Zealand						•		
USA						•	•	•
Canada						•		
Iceland						•	•	•
Estonia						•	•	•
Slovenia						•	•	•
The Philippines						•	•	•
Slovakia						•	•	•
Turkish Cypriot Community						•	•	
Nepal						•		
Lithuania							•	•
Russia							•	•
Serbia							•	•
Taiwan							•	
South Africa							•	•
Brazil								•
China								•
Croatia								•
Indonesia								•
Latvia								•
Romania								•

Source: *Cranet International Executive Report 2017.*

a result of contextual determinism, the role and impact of institutional actors, markets, and work regulation, the contextual specificities and dynamics in operation in the transition economies, along with key methodological challenges that arise when seeking to build cumulative comparative knowledge via network collaboration. By way of brief background and in order to underscore some of the themes central to the collaboration, we start with landscaping some of the associated critical developments that have previously been explored by the Network on aspects of each of these lines of inquiry, and we follow with an outline of the allied articles comprising this special issue.

Convergence and Contextualization in Comparative Perspective

A fundamental acceptance of the basic reality that obvious differences exist in the way HRM is conceptualized, institutionalized, and practiced, coupled with a belief in the academic value of empirically verifying the core architecture of HRM in a comparative way in each of the countries in the Network, became the wellspring for the establishment of Cranet at the outset. The underlying logic was rather modest, namely, that what operates successfully in one country may not be appropriate for another and, while importation of specific features of one system into another may occur, a blanket approach to the transposition appeared limited (Morley et al. 1996). In this way, the Network was joining a conversation that was emerging among a growing cohort of researchers who argued that context plays a critical role in the nature of HRM and that it is necessary to give expression to this pluralistic reality in conceiving our intercultural research models (Dewettinck and Remue 2011; Shapiro et al. 2007; Teagarden, Von Glinow, and Mellahi 2018; Tsui 2007; Von Glinow et al. 2002).

In addition, because of the nature of the Network and its consecutive waves of data collection, questions of continuity versus change and convergence versus divergence in preferred approaches and practices among different countries have, and continue to represent, a significant thread in the work of the Network collaborators (Brewster et al. 2000, 2004; Farndale et al. 2017; Mayrhofer et al. 2011). Writing of developments in the Network since its foundation, Parry, Stavrou-Costea, and Morley (2011, 3) note that "an exposition on patterns of convergence, or ongoing and enduring divergence evident from international, comparative and cross-cultural lines of enquiry has proven to be a significant cross cutting theme within the Network's research, and is beginning to emerge as an empirically testable proposition arising from the longitudinal nature of the Cranet Network." The convergence debate is focused on the issue of whether nation states, economies, and management practices are becoming more alike as a result of globalization. Cultural and institutional determinants of commonalities and differences in how HRM is implemented and practiced in different countries and territories have dominated the debate (Vaiman and Brewster 2015), the combination of which serve as the "rules of the game" governing the implementation of particular HRM practices and preferred approaches (Gooderham et al. 2015).

In particular, it has been argued that we need a more nuanced picture of convergence in HRM policies and practices. In this regard, Mayrhofer et al. (2011) distinguish between directional similarity which arises in situations where the analyzed variable changes in the same direction in each country, though there may have been significant variations in the starting level in each country, and final convergence which arises if the development of a variable in different countries points towards a common endpoint. In their empirical analysis of developments in HRM in larger private sector firms in 13 European countries between 1992 and 2004, they found considerable evidence of directional similarity with practices increasing or decreasing in the same way across the countries, but no evidence of final convergence, i.e., countries becoming more alike in the way they manage their people. In their more recent analysis, Farndale et al. (2017) explored patterns of HRM across market economies and between indigenous firms and foreign MNE subsidiary operations using Cranet data collected from nine countries at three points spanning a decade. They found that convergence and divergence occur to different extents in a nonlinear fashion and vary depending on the area of HRM practice observed. Thus, they found supporting evidence confirming that compensation and wage-bargaining level practices show more evidence of being institutionally constrained and, hence, were less likely to converge than, for example, HRM practices in the domain areas of contingent employment, training, and direct information provision. Their conclusions lend support to the contention surfaced by other Cranet collaborators that "although some convergence has been observed, different development trends, institutional determinants, cultural specificities, stakeholder preferences and relationships, rather than atrophying, have shown intractable resilience" (Lazarova et al. 2008,1995).

In our opening article in this issue titled "Context and HRM: Theory, Evidence, and Proposals," Wolfgang Mayrhofer, Paul Gooderham, and Chris Brewster build on the argument that HRM needs to take better account of context in order to more cogently explicate practice and outcome variability in HRM across countries. Reviewing studies produced from across the Cranet network of countries, and using comparative institutionalism as a theory of context that straddles levels of social complexity beyond national boundaries, they argue that the process of establishing and maintaining legitimacy for organizations is construed differently in different contexts. Citing theories of collective capitalisms that distinguish between liberal market economies (LMEs) and coordinated market economies (CMEs), and Business Systems theories, they demonstrate how institutional contexts constitute a powerful explanation for the use of HRM practices and outcomes and dispute arguments towards a convergence in HRM across country contexts. Rather, they posit that a comparative institutional perspective predicts significant differences across different contexts and the evidence to date from the Cranet data supports the thesis of limited convergence in HRM practices and outcomes. They conclude with a number of propositions to guide future evidence based research on contextual specificities across the global landscape.

Workplace Relations, Trade Unions and Financial Participation in Comparative Perspective

In the years since the Network was founded, the conversation on context, along with the importance of research approaches and accounts that capture context, have both grown in standing as prospective countermeasures to decontextualization in organizational behavior, HRM, and employment relations (Almond and Connolly 2019; Cooke 2018). It has been cogently argued that context "should be incorporated more mindfully and systematically into our research" (Johns 2017, 577), because it "permits integration across research areas and levels of analysis" (Johns 2018, 21). Such calls have made the case for contextualization at multiple levels because nuances "become apparent when we (a) purposefully introduce individual heterogeneity into the research model and (b) use context heterogeneity as a source of theorizing and avoid post hoc contextualization" (Minbaeva 2016, 95). Contextualization at the macro level is viewed as particularly critical in HRM because idiosyncratic elements of the institutional environment can strongly influence the development of formal structures, systems, and approaches in organizations, sometimes more profoundly than market pressures (Tregaskis, Heraty, and Morley 2001). Fundamentally, calls for deeper contextualization are an acknowledgement of the challenges that arise in "transporting social science models from one society to another" (Rousseau and Fried 2001, 1), along with the attendant importance of paying "special attention when exporting scientific constructs and research methodologies across national borders" (Rousseau and Fried 2001, 2).

Parry, Stavrou-Costea, and Morley (2011, 2) argue that Cranet in particular speaks to the issue of contextualization and its importance through "advancing research in different socio-cultural contexts." They contend that this has been a particularly important strength of the Network. A hugely diverse range of countries, from advanced economies to emerging ones (several of which have rarely featured in the English language literature heretofore), have been landscaped in terms of HRM by the Network and have been provided "with a platform through which they can communicate to the international scientific community the nature of legitimate practice in their respective countries" (2). Through long-term collaboration between research partners in participating countries engaging in sequential, longitudinal research, and through the subsequent curating of the research insights generated, the Network facilitates an "exposition of systems and content and national patterns of HRM as a result of the distinctive developmental paths of different countries and their subsequently idiosyncratic institutional and economic regimes" (Lazarova, Morley, and Tyson 2008).

From a contemporary perspective, contextualization remains especially important because of on-going large scale changes in the social, political, legal, and economic climate of many countries which have brought with them significant alterations to the nature of the relationship between key stakeholders including government, employers, and trade unions. This has prompted a significant debate on the ramifications for work and workplace relations. While there have been some suggestions of it heralding something of a sea change in the industrial relations landscape, there remains considerable disagreement over the nature and extent of the current transformation and an acknowledgement that the response to emerging pressures is far from uniform across countries.

Picking up on this debate, in their article titled "A Comparative Study of Trade Union Influence in Spanish and Brazilian Firms: The Role of Industrial Relations Systems and Their Historical Evolution," Wilson Aparecido Costa de Amorim, Andre Luiz Fischer, and Jordi Trullen present a comparative study of trade union influence in Spanish and Brazilian firms with an explicit focus on industrial relations systems. They suggest a timeliness to such a comparative study given the recent rise in what they describe as anti-union attitudes in two countries that are characterized by strong collectivist traditions and where trade unions are long recognized as legitimate stakeholders in work related debates and national negotiations. Moreover, strike activity has increased significantly in recent years in both countries. Drawing on date from the 2014 Cranet survey, the authors explore the presence and perceived influence of trade unions in both Spanish and Brazilian-based organizations. The data suggest that union membership is low by international standards in both countries, and their presence at local level is not felt strongly by managers in day-to-day activities. However, national collective bargaining arrangements provide a legitimate means through which unions are able to influence important working conditions, including pay and hours of work in both countries. Trade unions played a strong and often politicized role in movements towards establishing democracy in both countries and this legacy has conferred legitimacy for continued institutional shaping of the national system for labor governance and social action. There are some marked differences between the countries in terms of individualized practices, such as interactions with works councils, or communication with employees through trade union channels. Here the authors contend that the national industrial relations system determines many of the practices that are in evidence at the local level. For example, trade unions emerged and operate at the national level and primarily for collective bargaining purposes in Brazil and, thus, appear to have little, if any, influence at the organizational level; by comparison, trade unions in Spain have a mandate at both the national and the local level, and their presence shapes more organizational exchanges and practices through works councils. The authors conclude that the national industrial relations system confers a distinctive role on trade unions and this institutional feature then shapes the extent to which their influence has a direct or indirect influence on local organizational practices.

Michael Brooks, Geoffrey Wood, and Chris Brewster in their article titled "The Antecedents of Comparative Differences in Union Presence and Engagement: Evidence From Coordinated and Liberal Market Contexts" explore the antecedents of comparative differences in union representation and employer engagement with them at the workplace level in an effort to determine whether there is evidence of a shift towards non-unionism across larger organization in different institutional contexts. Drawing on arguments that national institutional factors exert differential effects on national employment relations practices, they question whether union presence, and the willingness of employers to engage formally with them, is a function of the macro environment in which they operate. Referencing an overall general decline in union density across institutional settings in many studies to date, they explore whether there is evidence of large scale and converging changes in union membership and representation within distinct economies, or rather more modest and context distinctive patterns of union membership and presence in different economies.

Drawing on data from five rounds of the Cranet studies in three countries (UK, Germany, and Sweden), that represent distinct economy types (liberal market economy, coordinated market economy, and social democratic capitalism, respectively), their analysis shows that, while there has been some decline in union representation and the extent of employer engagement with them, important national differences persist between countries and economies. Different types of economies were found to be distinct in terms of representation, but variation was also found within economies themselves. The authors conclude that although union membership is on the decline, the rates of decline vary across and within the economies studied and, so, there was no evidence to suggest a convergence in union related practices. They posited that context continues to mold both the incidence of unions and collective bargaining and mitigate (or accelerate) their decline.

In their article titled "Understanding Financial Participation Across Market Economies," Elaine Farndale, J. Ryan Lamare, Maja Vidović, and Amar S. Chauhan explore corporate practice in financial participation in 4,253 organizations across 19 Cranet countries through a varieties of capitalism lens to demonstrate whether and how institutional constraints at the market economy level influence the range of organizational level financial participation choices and offerings. Focusing on equity ownership and profit sharing specifically, as additive (non-mandated) schemes that may be used to motivate employees, they consider a range of broad institutional factors that may lead firms to adopt such practices, or constrain their choices to so do. They apply a comparative capitalisms theoretical framework, wherein countries are categorized into five different market economies according to both the patterns of institutional arrangements in evidence and strategic interactions between the different institutional players in that economy. Focusing on three particular institutional markets that are most likely to impact financial participation (product, financial, and labor markets, respectively), the authors argue that the take-up of financial participation is likely to vary considerably across these economies as firms strive to align their strategies to their institutional country context to achieve legitimacy. Their analysis confirmed that the use of financial participation schemes was indeed influenced by economic, regulatory, and market forces operating at the macro context of the firm, and with some evidence of isomorphism wherein different patterns of adoption and diffusion were evident in the different market economies. They conclude that the market economy level of analysis is an important variable in explaining financial participation usage, in addition to extant organizational and country level considerations, and that organizations operating across market economics give due consideration to the influence of such institutional arrangements on management practice.

HRM in the Transition Economies in Comparative Perspective

Cooke (2018, 2) argues that the globalized economy has led to a number of developments, not least the "the diffusion, albeit partial, and often with adaptation, of various western-originated management concepts and techniques in (less developed) host countries with different institutional environment and cultural traditions." To aid the deepening of our understanding of the emerging economies as contexts for enquiry, it has been argued that they should not simply represent new locations for imposing Western approaches and solutions, but should themselves serve as the wellspring for novel ideas, grounded in local long-standing legitimacy which can and should more fully inform the body of knowledge (Horwitz, Budhwar, and Morley 2015).

Heretofore, a suite of academic articles from the Cranet Network have focused on landscaping various aspects of HRM in the transition economies of Central and Eastern Europe and the Former Soviet Union, partly as a response to the fact that these territories have been historically underrepresented in the literature and partly because, as economies in transition, a longitudinal collaborative network is well placed to observe the nature, direction, and consequences of such transitions (Berber et al. 2017; Brewster, Morley, and Bučiuniene 2010; Bučiuniene and Kazlauskaite 2012; Garavan et al. 1998; Gurkov and Zelenova 2011; Gurkov, Zelenova, and Saidov 2012; Karoliny, Farkas, and Poór 2009; Morley et al. 2016; Poór et al. 2011; Vanhala, Kaarelson, and Alas 2006).

Since the fall of the Berlin Wall the words "transition" and "transformation" have become synonymous with Central and Eastern Europe and the Former Soviet Union (Morley, Minbaeva, and Michailova 2018), and the observing of the transitions and the recording and reporting of developments in HRM at system and organizational level in these countries has been a key focus of activity (Morley et al. 2016, 2009). The early discourse on transition in these countries was dominated by economic accounts of the events, with broader social impact accounts subsequently following. Sakowski, Vadi, and Merikül (2015, 76) suggest that "the process of transition, in the sense of the changeover, has been completed for some time," while the process of "shaping society continues and still affects the organizational formation and functioning of organizations today." Nonetheless, transition economies remain complex and idiosyncratic, relative to their western counterparts when it comes to the establishment of socially legitimate management policies and practices, in part at least because of ongoing ideational legacies arising from historical exigencies and because of country specific endowments (Berend 1996). Added to this, the increased numbers of foreign multinational companies in the region post-transition have emerged as "shapers of institutional environments and purveyors of particular governance mechanisms and practices." These typically emanate from economically dominant countries of origin and increasingly diffuse their practices to subsidiaries in emerging markets and territories. Their scale and presence has resulted in diverging developmental trajectories in terms of the type of market economy pursued by each country.

Meyer and Peng (2016:4) note that the geographic entity of Central and Eastern Europe as a territory may not now be as theoretically meaningful as it was in earlier years of the transition process because of the divergence of countries in the region during the transition and the convergence of some countries in the region with others outside of it. In their article for this Special Issue, titled "Contemporary Human Resource Management Practices in Russia: Flexibility Under Uncertainty," Veronika Kabalina, Olga Zelenova, and Kira Reshetnikova provide a fresh account of developments in HRM in Russia since the transition process. They draw on Cranet data from a Russian sample to identify a core set of what they describe as flexibly oriented HRM practices (FHRMP) that can allow for adaptation to a turbulent business and institutional environment. Described in terms of both variety of HRM methods available to them, and line function autonomy in decision-making and/or outsourcing, flexibility in HRM practices and offerings is considered a critical feature for management in transitioning economies characterized by cycles of crisis and reform. Russia is a pertinent exemplar here, where flexibility has been established as a key characteristic of the Russian labor market since 1992. The authors identify a core set of FHRMPs that straddle staffing, training and development, pay, and employment relations practices, and which are then indexed to indicate minimum, medium, and maximum flexibility. Environmental uncertainty was measured by both complexity and dynamism in the internal and external environments. The authors found that flexibility among Russian organizations measured closest to the medium level, with greater flexibility evident in practices concerned with development than with staffing or compensation, for example. There was some evidence of greater flexibility being formed in more complex environments, and particularly among organizations that compete in global markets. There was no observed correlation between dynamism and flexibility—the authors posit that this could be attributed to organizational inertia or an unwillingness to embrace more wholesale change.

Methodological Challenges in Building Cumulative Comparative Knowledge in HRM

The final article in this Special Issue calls attention to methodological challenges underlying the co-production of knowledge via international cooperative research networks, and in so doing, it echoes a long standing debate in the literature on comparative management research (Clark, Grant, and Heijltjes 1999; Teagarden et al. 1995). Of note in the case of Cranet, methodological debates on the conducting and reporting of international comparative research have occupied a critical place in the Network's discourse since its inception in 1989, as indeed have the co-ordination and the control mechanisms that operate in the governance and maintenance of the Network itself (Brewster, Mayrhofer, and Reichel 2011; Mayrhofer 1998; Steinmetz et al. 2011).

Our final article by Jesper Christensen, Frans Bévort, and Erling Rasmussen, titled "The Cranet Survey: Improving on a Challenged Research Practice?" continues in this tradition of explicating the methodological challenges that arise in building comparative knowledge from the research effort of a cross-country collaborative network. They explore the challenges of working with a longitudinal survey, such as Cranet, that is designed to balance the sometimes competing requirements for standardization with adaptation to account for differentiation in HRM practices across countries. Using a comparative analysis of the rate of professionalization in both Denmark and New Zealand as a backdrop, the authors chart what they describe as the research practice of administering a longitudinal survey and developing a systemized database for comparative purposes. Introducing the concepts of variance identification and variance distribution, the authors demonstrate how researchers can successfully navigate the standardization/differentiation tradeoff without compromising methodological rigor and data comparability. Variance identification refers to the inevitable discontinuities that arise in research team membership and activities over long periods of time, while variance distribution concerns managing the idiosyncratic survey variations and sampling strategies across and within countries. The article describes the stages involved in developing and maintaining a common research design across countries, with sufficient flexibility to account for trends and developments in HRM over time, and idiosyncratic country or culture variations. They argue that the long term validity is determined by the identification and management of variations in data over time, within the network, and across countries, in order to produce appropriate knowledge management and decision frameworks for research teams. They explain the challenges that are posed in this endeavor and how best to overcome measurement error, sampling inconsistencies and indeed definitional discontinuities.

REFERENCES

Almond, P., and H. Connolly. 2019. "A Manifesto for 'Slow' Comparative Research on Work and Employment." *European Journal of Industrial Relations* :095968011983416. doi:10.1177/0959680119834164.

Berber, N., M. J. Morley, A. Slavić, and J. Poór. 2017. "Management Compensation Systems in Central and Eastern Europe: A Comparative Analysis." *The International Journal of Human Resource Management* 28 (12):1661–89. doi:10.1080/09585192.2016.1277364.

Berend, T. 1996. *Central and Eastern Europe, 1944–1993: Detour from the Periphery to the Periphery.* Cambridge: Cambridge University Press.

Bournois, F., and F. Chevalier. 1998. "Doing Research with Foreign Colleagues: A Project Life-Cycle Approach." *Journal of Managerial Psychology* 13 (3/4):206–13. doi:10.1108/02683949810215011.

Brewster, C., W. Mayrhofer, and M. Morley. 2000. *New Challenges for European Human Resource Management.* Basingstoke: Macmillan.

Brewster, C., W. Mayrhofer, and M. Morley. 2004. *Human Resource Management in Europe: Evidence of Convergence?* Oxford: Elsevier Butterworth-Heinemann.

Brewster, C., W. Mayrhofer, and A. Reichel. 2011. "Riding *the Tiger*? Going along with Cranet for Two Decades – a Relational Perspective." *Human Resource Management Review* 21 (1):5–15. doi:10.1016/j.hrmr.2010.09.007.

Brewster, C., M. J., Morley, and I. Bučiuniene. 2010. "The Reality of Human Resource Management in Central and Eastern Europe: A Special Issue to Mark the 20th Anniversary of Cranet (the Cranfield Network) on Comparative Human Resource." *Baltic Journal of Management.* 5 (2):145–55. doi:10.1108/17465261011045098.

Bučiuniene, I., and R. Kazlauskaite. 2012. "The Linkage between HRM, CSR and Performance Outcomes." *Baltic Journal of Management* 7 (1):5–24.

Clark, T., D. Grant, and M. Heijltjes. 1999. "Researching Comparative and International Human Resource Management." *International Studies of Management & Organization* 29 (4):6–23. doi:10.1080/00208825.1999.11656773.

Cooke, F. L. 2018. "Concepts, Contexts, and Mind-Sets: Putting Human Resource Management Research in Perspectives." *Human Resource Management Journal* 28 (1):1–13. doi:10.1111/1748-8583.12163.

Cooke, F. L., A. Veen, and G. Wood. 2017. "What Do We Know about Cross-Country Comparative Studies in HRM? a Critical Review of Literature in the Period of 2000–2014." *The International Journal of Human Resource Management* 28 (1):196–233. doi:10.1080/09585192.2016.1245671.

Dewettinck, K., and J. Remue. 2011. "Contextualizing HRM in Comparative Research: The Role of the Cranet Network." *Human Resource Management Review* 21 (1):37–49. doi:10.1016/j.hrmr.2010.09.010.

Easterby-Smith, M., and D. Malina. 1999. "Cross-Cultural Collaborative Research: Towards Reflexivity." *Academy of Management Journal* 42 (1):76–86. doi:10.5465/256875.

Farndale, E., P. Ligthart, E. Poutsma, and C. Brewster. 2017. "The Effects of Market Economy Type and Foreign MNE Subsidiaries on the Convergence and Divergence of HRM." *Journal of International Business Studies* 48 (9):1065–86. doi:10.1057/s41267-017-0094-8.

Garavan, T., M. J. Morley, N. Heraty, J. Lucewicz, and A. Suchodolski. 1998. "Managing Human Resources in a Post-Command Economy: Personnel Administration or Strategic HRM." *Personnel Review* 27 (3):200–12. doi:10.1108/00483489810210606.

Geringer, M. J., C. A. Frayne, and J. F. Milliman. 2002. "In Search of "Best Practices" in International Human Resource Management: Research Design and Methodology." *Human Resource Management* 41 (1):5–30. doi:10.1002/hrm.10017.

Gooderham, P. N., M. J. Morley, E. Parry, and E. Stavrou. 2015. "National and Firm-Level Drivers of the Devolution of HRM Decision Making to Line Managers." *Journal of International Business Studies* 46 (6): 715–23. doi:10.1057/jibs.2015.5.

Gurkov, I., and O. Zelenova. 2011. "Human Resource Management in Russian Companies." *International Studies of Management & Organization* 41 (4):65–78. doi:10.2753/IMO0020-8825410404.

Gurkov, I., O. Zelenova, and Z. Saidov. 2012. "Mutation of HRM Practices in Russia: An Application of CRANET Methodology." *The International Journal of Human Resource Management* 23 (7):1289–302. doi:10.1080/09585192.2011.581633.

Horwitz, F., P. Budhwar, and M. J. Morley. 2015. "Future Trends in Human Resource Management in Emerging Markets". In *Handbook of Human Resource Management in Emerging Markets.*, eds. F Horwitz and P Budhwar, 470–88. Cheltenham, UK: Edward Elgar.

House, Robert, Mansour Javidan, Paul Hanges, and Peter Dorfman. 2002. "Understanding Cultures and Implicit Leadership Theories across the Globe: An Introduction to Project GLOBE." *Journal of World Business* 37 (1): 3–10. doi:10.1016/S1090-9516(01)00069-4.

Jackson, T. 2013. "Reconstructing the Indigenous in African Management Research." *Management International Review* 53 (1):13–38. doi:10.1007/s11575-012-0161-0.

Johns, G. 2017. "Reflections on the 2016 Decade Award: Incorporating Context in Organizational Research." *Academy of Management Review* 42 (4):577–95. doi:10.5465/amr.2017.0044.

Johns, G. 2018. "Advances in the Treatment of Context in Organizational Research." *Annual Review of Organizational Psychology and Organizational Behavior* 5 (1):21–46. doi:10.1146/annurev-orgpsych-032117-104406.

Jonsen, K., C. L. Butler, K. Makela, R. Piekkari, R. Drogendijk, J. Lauring, J. E. Lervik, C. Pahlberg, M. Vodosek, and L. Zander. 2013. "Processes of International Collaboration in Management Research: A Reflexive, Auto-Ethnographic Approach." *Journal of Management Inquiry* 22 (4):394–413. doi:10.1177/1056492612464429.

Karoliny, Z., F. Farkas, and J. Poór. 2009. "In Focus: Hungarian and Central Eastern European Characteristics of Human Resource Management: An International Comparative Survey." *Journal of East European Management Studies* 14 (1):9–47. doi:10.5771/0949-6181-2009-1-9.

Lazarova, M., M. J. Morley, and S. Tyson. 2008. "International Comparative Studies in HRM and Performance – the Cranet Data." *The International Journal of Human Resource Management* 19 (11):1995–2003. doi:10.1080/09585190802404239.

Leung, K. 2012. "Indigenous Chinese Management Research: Like It or Not, We Need It." *Management and Organization Review* 8 (1):1–5. doi:10.1111/j.1740-8784.2012.00288.x.

Lowrie, A., and P. J. McKnight. 2004. "Academic Research Networks: A Key to Enhancing Scholarly Standing." *European Management Journal* 22 (4):345–60. doi:10.1016/j.emj.2004.06.011.

Mayrhofer, W. 1998. "Between Market, Bureaucracy and Clan: Coordination and Control Mechanisms in the Cranfield Network on European Human Resource Management (Cranet-E)." *Journal of Managerial Psychology* 13 (3/4):241–58. doi:10.1108/02683949810215057.

Mayrhofer, W., C. Brewster, M. J. Morley, and J. Ledolter. 2011. "Hearing a Different Drummer? Convergence of Human Resource Management in Europe – a Longitudinal Analysis." *Human Resource Management Review* 21 (1):50–67. doi:10.1016/j.hrmr.2010.09.011.

Meyer, K., and M. Peng. 2016. "Theoretical Foundations of Emerging Economy Business Research." *Journal of International Business Studies* 47 (1):3–22. doi:10.1057/jibs.2015.34.

Minbaeva, D. 2016. "Contextualising the Individual in International Management Research: Black Boxes, Comfort Zones and a Future Research Agenda." *European J. Of International Management* 10 (1):95–104. doi:10.1504/EJIM.2016.073990.

Morley, M. J., C. Brewster, P. Gunnigle, and W. Mayrhofer 1996. "Evaluating Change in European Industrial Relations: Research Evidence on Trends at Organisational Level." *The International Journal of Human Resource Management* 7 (3):640–57. doi:10.1080/09585199600000148.

Morley, M. J., N. Heraty, and S. Michailova. 2009. *Managing Human Resources in Central and Eastern Europe.* London: Routledge.

Morley, M. J., J. Poór, N. Heraty, R. Alas, and A. Pocztowski. 2016. "Developments in Human Resource Management in Central and Eastern Europe in Comparative Perspective." In *Contemporary Human Resource Issues in Europe.*, eds. M. Dickmann, C. Brewster and P. Sparrow, 73–99. London: Routledge.

Morley, M. J., A. Slavić, J. Poór, and N. Berber. 2016. "Training Practices and Organisational Performance: A Comparative Analysis of Domestic and International Market Oriented Organisations in Central & Eastern Europe." *Journal of East European Management Studies* 21 (4):406–32. doi:10.5771/0949-6181-2016-4-406.

Morley, M. J., D. Minbaeva, and S. Michailova. 2018. "HRM in the Transition States of Central and Eastern Europe and the former Soviet Union." In *Handbook of Research on Comparative Human Resource Management. (*2nd Ed*)*, eds. C. Brewster, W. Mayrhofer and Elaine Farndale, 469–86. Cheltenham: Edward Elgar Publishing.

Parry., E., E. Stavrou-Costea, and M. J. Morley. 2011. "The Cranet International Research Network on Human Resource Management in Retrospect and Prospect." *Human Resource Management Review* 21 (1):1–4. doi:10. 1016/j.hrmr.2010.09.006.

Poór, J., Z. Karoliny, R. Alas, and E. Vtchkova. 2011. "Comparative International Human Resource Management in the Light of the Cranet Regional Research Survey in Transitional Economies." *Employee Relations* 33 (4): 428–43. doi:10.1108/01425451111142710.

Rigby, J., and J. Edler. 2005. "Peering inside Research Networks: Some Observations on the Effect of the Intensity of Collaboration on the Variability of Research Quality." *Research Policy* 34 (6):784–94. doi:10.1016/j.respol. 2005.02.004.

Rousseau, D. M., and Y. Fried. 2001. "Location, Location, Location: Contextualizing Organizational Research." *Journal of Organizational Behavior* 22 (1):1–13. doi:10.1002/job.78.

Sakowski, K., M. Vadi, and J. Meriküll. 2015. "Formalization of Organizational Structure as a Subject of Path Dependency: An Example from Central and Eastern Europe." *Post-Communist Economies* 27 (1):76–90. doi:10. 1080/14631377.2015.992229.

Shapiro, D. L., M. A. Von Glinow, and Z. Xiao. 2007. "Toward Poly-Contextually Sensitive Research Methods." *Management and Organization Review* 3 (1):129–52. doi:10.1111/j.1740-8784.2007.00058.x.

Steinmetz, H., C. Schwens, M. Wehner, and R. Kabst. 2011. "Conceptual and Methodological Issues in Comparative HRM Research: The Cranet Project as an Example." *Human Resource Management Review* 21 (1): 16–26. doi:10.1016/j.hrmr.2010.09.008.

Teagarden, M., M. A. Von Glinow, and K. Mellahi. 2018. "Contextualising International Business Research: Enhancing Rigor and Relevance." *Journal of World Business* 53 (3):303–6. doi:10.1016/j.jwb. 2017.09.001.

Teagarden, M. A., M. A. Von Glinow, D. Bowen, C. Frayne, S. Nason, Y. Paul Huo, J. Milliman, M. Arias, M. Butler, J. Michael Geringer, et al. 1995. "Towards a Theory of Comparative Management Research: An Idiographic Case Study of the Best International Human Resource Management Project." *Academy of Management Journal* 38 (5):1261–87. doi:10.2307/256857.

Tregaskis, O., N. Heraty, and M. J. Morley. 2001. "HRD in Multinationals: The Global/Local Mix." *Human Resource Management Journal* 11 (2):34–56. doi:10.1111/j.1748-8583.2001.tb00037.x.

Tsui, A. 2007. "From Homogenization to Pluralism: International Management Research in the Academy and Beyond." *Academy of Management Journal* 50 (6):1353–64. doi:10.5465/amj.2007.28166121.

Tung, R. L., and Z. Aycan. 2008. "Key Success Factors and Indigenous Management Practices in SMEs in Emerging Economies." *Journal of World Business* 43 (4):381–4. doi:10.1016/j.jwb.2008.04.001.

Vaiman, V., and C. Brewster. 2015. "How Far Do Cultural Differences Explain the Differences between Nations? Implications for HRM." *The International Journal of Human Resource Management* 26 (2):151–64. doi:10.1080/ 09585192.2014.937969.

Vanhala, S., T. Kaarelson, and R. Alas. 2006. "Converging Human Resource Management: A Comparison between Estonia and Finnish HRM." *Baltic Journal of Management* 1 (1):82–101. doi:10.1108/ 17465260610640895.

Von Glinow, M. A., E. A. Drost, and M. B. Teagarden. 2002. "Converging on IHRM Best Practices: Lessons Learned from a Globally Distributed Consortium on Theory and Practice." *Human Resource Management* 41 (1): 123–40. doi:10.1002/hrm.10023.

Context and HRM: Theory, Evidence, and Proposals

Wolfgang Mayrhofer, Paul N. Gooderham and Chris Brewster

Abstract: Human resource management (HRM) has paid insufficient attention to the impact of context. In this article, we outline the need for HRM to take full account of context, particularly national context, and to use both cultural theories and, particularly, institutional theories to do that. We use research publications that utilize the Cranet data to show how that can be done. From that evidence, we develop a series of proposals for further context-based research in HRM.

INTRODUCTION

Human Resource Management (HRM) has paid insufficient attention to the impact of context. There are clear reasons for that and also clear weaknesses that result from it. So we outline the need for HRM to take proper account of context. Whilst conscious of the importance of what we might call the organization's proximate context (for example, its technology, its competitive position, and its success) and of what we might call the intermediate levels of context (such as size and sector), here we focus particularly on the more encompassing levels of national context: the national context and international clusters within which the organization operates. Whilst we believe that doing so requires the use of both cultural theories and institutional theories, and we concentrate on the latter, since we believe that the latter can to some extent encompass culture ("soft institutions"), that measures of national culture remain

---

inconsistent (Avloniti and Filippaios 2014) and that organizations have limited ability to "work around" institutional constraints compared to cultural ones (Vaiman and Brewster 2015). We use research publications that utilize the Cranet data* to show how that can be done. From that evidence, we develop a series of proposals for further context-based research in HRM.

Because this is a review article, rather than a report on a specific research project, its format is a little unusual. First, we clarify what we mean by HRM and briefly develop a critique of the extant research as largely ignoring the importance of context. We then consider comparative institutionalism as a theory of context. Thereafter, we present evidence drawn from the Cranet network exploring and explaining differences in HRM in Europe to show how significant context is for HRM practices and outcomes. In the penultimate section, we review Cranet evidence that there is no significant convergence of national systems of HRM practices, suggesting that context remains a potent explanatory factor over time. Finally, we draw on the first two sections of the article to suggest a series of propositions for future research.

The Cranfield Network on International Human Resource Management (IHRM) (Cranet), was established to meet the need for ready access to information on best practice and comparative performance within Europe and, now, globally. Cranet is now an established research collaboration between over 40 universities and business schools with a proven track record of collecting powerful, representative data, on a continuing basis; undertaking rigorous analysis and disseminating high quality results.

THEORIES OF HUMAN RESOURCE MANAGEMENT (HRM)

According to Schuler and Jackson (2005), the study of HRM started in the United States in the mid-1970s as a response to the increasing professionalization of HRM by HRM specialists, and a growing recognition of the importance of human resources to companies' success. As a consequence, businesses in the United States began to view human resource professionals as partners "who should be involved in the strategic decision making processes of the firm" (Schuler and Jackson 2005,12). The subject was encapsulated in two "founding" texts that appeared at the same time in the early 1980s (Kaufman 2015). These offered approaches developed in two of the leading University Management Schools in the United States: one by Beer et al. (1984), offering the "Harvard model," and one by Fombrun, Tichy, and Devanna (1984) offering the "Chicago model" of HRM. The "Harvard" map of the territory of HRM, as they termed it, took a wider perspective, giving a prominent role to stakeholder interests, long-term consequences, and "situational factors." Situational factors, or what we call context, were not a feature of the Fombrun et al. (1984) text. Instead, it was significantly tightly concentrated on the HRM chain within the firm as a means to promoting performance, and was prescriptive, recommending systematic use of strategically based selection, individual performance appraisal, individual performance-related rewards, and outcomes-monitored training and development. The approach is unitarist, in the sense that employers and employees are not viewed as having conflicting or divergent interests (Walton 1985) and other stakeholders' interests are not relevant, so firms are, or should be, able to develop their HRM practices free of industrial relations or governmental pressures. As Sparrow and Hiltrop

(1994, 7) phrased it, in terms of this HRM paradigm, human resources are "to be obtained cheaply, used sparingly, and developed and exploited as fully as possible in accordance with the demands determined by the overall business strategy."

The notion of HRM quickly spread to Europe and then around the world. One reason for that was the lack of construct clarity around the phrase so that researchers with different approaches could all cheerfully claim to be discussing HRM. Whist this led to a number of critiques in the UK press in particular (Guest 1990; Legge 1995), in practice the Fombrun et al. approach to HRM rapidly became the dominant paradigm. Purely in terms of citations, the most cited HRM journal articles deal with the impact of elements of the HRM chain on organizational performance. However, of greater significance to our argument is that the focus is on firms within single national contexts, overwhelmingly that of the United States. As such, context has not been considered to matter. Whilst, as we note below, since these early days there have been calls for context to be taken into account in our explanations of HRM policy and practice, and there has been some research that does that, the role of context, and particularly nation context, remains a minority concern amongst HRM researchers. As a range of complaints have made clear (Rynes, Brown, and Colbert 2002; Rynes, Giluk, and Brown 2007), this lack of context is one reason why practitioners are not "listening" to the researchers. The dominant strand of HRM ignores the everyday experience of practitioners who are always conscious of context and the need to satisfy a complex range of internal and external stakeholders whose interests are not necessarily compatible.

Context

More recently it has been recognized in HRM, and specifically in IHRM (see, e.g., Delbridge, Hauptmeier, and Sengupta 2011), that a weakness in much of the extant "strategic" literature is that it rests on a fundamental assumption that managements can choose and implement any strategy that they deem appropriate (Wangrow, Schepker, and Barker 2015), and further, that the strategies they implement will have direct and intended consequences regardless of context.

The HRM research that is most likely to overcome these weaknesses views management action as nested within enabling and constraining forces, so that management can maneuver only within relatively tight, externally located limits. Hence, a simplistic focus on the HRM chain of policies, practices, and perceptions (Wright and Nishii 2013) and the corporate strategy or policies of the firm misses important factors. Organization operates in context. As Beer et al. (1984) noted, context includes external stakeholders, such as economic actors, governments, local authorities, and trade unions, and background factors, such as the size and economic power of the country, its history, and the levels of economic development, and the rule of law interact to set the framework within which the organization operates. These all impact the HRM chain within the organization, and the outcomes of that chain are located at different levels of social complexity: outcomes for the individual employee; for organizational HRM; for organizational results; for the community; and the country.

Comparative Theories

In this article, we address comparative HRM and the level of context that occurs at, and above, national level. We accept that factors, such as the size of the organization and the sector in which it operates are important, and we do not deny the importance of the organization's competitive situation, but our interest is in context at the national level and above. Conceptualizing context requires defining a theoretical angle. The descriptive use of "obvious surface phenomena," such as size, sector, unemployment rates, or quality of the educational system, is important but has its limits. Unless we define what these elements represent in theoretical terms, understanding their importance for HRM is difficult. There are two basic sets of theories that have been used to explain differences in management generally and HRM in particular at this level (Brewster and Mayrhofer 2012), namely, cultural theories and institutional theories. Both are important to get a full picture of HRM, and we note some examples of the culturally based literature below. Our main attention, though, is given to institutional theories, since we believe that in many cases managements can "navigate around" cultural differences, since they can, for example, recruit people who do not fit the local cultural stereotypes into a subsidiary, but they have much less autonomy with regard to institutions, such as the law or fiscal regulations, where they are constrained to either obey the rules or risk severe penalties (Vaiman and Brewster 2015). Hoffmann (1999, 351) states that, "[i]nstitutional theory directs attention toward forces that lie beyond the organizational boundary, in the realm of social processes (Powell and DiMaggio 1991; Scott 1995)". A firm's action is seen not as a choice among an unlimited array of possibilities determined by purely internal arrangements, but rather as a choice among a narrowly defined set of legitimate options determined by the group of actors composing the firm's *organizational field* (Scott 1991). The form of this influence is manifested in *institutions:* rules, norms, and beliefs that describe reality for the organization, explaining what is and what is not, what can be acted upon and what cannot. The field of comparative (neo-)institutionalism argues that to be effective, organizations must establish and maintain legitimacy, and notes that this is construed differently in different national settings.

There have been approaches that focus on single institutional elements, and these have been used by Cranet authors, as we note below. Thus, analysts have attempted to link intra-organizational behavior with national politics (Roe 2003), political systems (Pagano and Volpin 2005), or legislation (Botero et al. 2004). Botero et al. (2004), for example, focus on the role labor regulation plays in determining management practices, and Botero et al. (2004, 1339) contend that "every country in the world has established a complex system of laws and institutions intended to protect the interests of workers." Further, they argue that systems of labor regulation constitute formal institutions that constrain the actions of firms, their managers, and employees through rewarding or sanctioning particular courses of behavior. The most promising and to date widely used approach in HRM are the synthetic theories developed to include these and other national factors in explaining the differences between countries. Collectively, these are known as theories of comparative capitalisms (Jackson and Deeg 2008).

Comparative capitalisms encompass theories of Varieties of Capitalism (Hall and Soskice 2001; Thelen 2014), which draw a distinction between the Liberal Market Economies (LMEs) of the English-speaking world and the Coordinated Market Economies (CMEs) of, mainly, the Rhineland countries. LMEs are "shareholder economies," where competition is key, and is legislatively required, and in which private enterprise is about maximizing short-term profits for the owners of the business. Government's role is to "hold the field" but otherwise not interfere with business. In the CMEs there is more coordination through relational contracting, coordination, and mutual monitoring through networks. Firms collaborate with each other and with government and pay attention to a wider set of stakeholders. These differences apply within the firm too. In LMEs, managements and unions compete, while in CMEs they are more likely to collaborate, reinforced by legislation on employee rights and by financial arrangements that are less reliant on open capital markets. Other authors under the comparative capitalisms rubric have given their theories different titles and identified different categories (Amable 2003; Whitley 1999) but are similarly focused on explaining firm actions through the context in which they operate.

In firms operating in the CME context, managements are significantly more institutionally constrained than those in the LME context, in the sense that they operate within legal frameworks and systems of industrial relations that limit their autonomy in applying market-driven or technologically contingent management practices. Hall and Soskice (2001) point to a number of systemic differences in HRM practices between firms operating in LMEs and CMEs. Thus, whereas in LMEs there are substantial pay differentials, even within the same industries, in CMEs most pay negotiation occurs at the industry level, taking pay negotiation out of the workplace. Likewise, whereas in LMEs the opportunities for employee dismissal for economic reasons are relatively unconstrained, in CMEs there is a tradition of long-term labor contracts and substantially greater security against arbitrary lay-offs.

Hall and Soskice (2001) recognize that there are a large number of countries that fall outside of their analysis. Both Amable (2003) and Whitley (1999), amongst others, cover a wider range of countries and have more to say about relationships within the organization than Hall and Soskice. Common to all of these approaches is that certain institutional contexts provide managers with greater autonomy than others. Using studies employing comparative institutional theory and data from Cranet surveys, we shall show how context constitutes a powerful explanation of the use of HRM practices and outcomes. The Cranet survey was developed in order to test not only elements of the Chicago model (e.g., performance-related compensation) but also the Harvard model (e.g., employee voice).

While some Cranet studies have included the effects of national culture (e.g., Nikandrou et al. 2008), the overall theoretical thrust of Cranet research has been located within comparative institutional theory. Thus, there have been Cranet studies using varieties of capitalism (Hall and Soskice 2001; Thelen 2014) and business systems (Amable 2003; Whitley 1999) amongst others. Perhaps the most comprehensive test of such theories has been applied by Walker, Brewster, and Wood (2014). Using internal firm-level evidence that market economies (largely on the Amable models) are distinctive in terms of HRM, they find considerable diversity within them but significantly that there are more differences between the varieties than there are within them.

THE CONTINUING IMPORTANCE OF CONTEXT?

First, however, we address the question of whether analyses based on national context remain important. The thrust of the arguments that globalization increasingly affects every aspect of business (Drori, Meyer, and Hwang 2006; Gospel and Pendleton 2005) is that HRM may become increasingly standardized to a dominant, efficient model of "best practice." In brief, the convergence thesis argues that differences in management systems, which have arisen as a result of the geographical isolation of businesses, and the consequent development of differing beliefs and value orientations of national cultures, are being superseded by the logic of technology and markets that requires the adoption of specific, and, therefore, universally applicable, management techniques (Kidger 1991).

In direct contrast, proponents of the divergence thesis argue that personnel management systems, far from being economically or technologically derived, epitomize national contexts that do not respond readily to the imperatives of technology or the market. According to this perspective, organizational choice is limited by culture and by institutional pressures, including the state, regulatory structures, interest groups, public opinion, and norms (DiMaggio and Powell 1983; Meyer and Rowan 1983; Oliver 1991). Moreover, many of these pressures are so accepted, so taken-for-granted "as to be invisible to the actors they influence" (Oliver 1991, 148). Alternatively, it has been argued that the embeddedness of HRM means that it is likely to remain distinct in each country (Brewster and Mayrhofer 2012; Meyer, Mudambi, and Narula 2011).

While many researchers have been constrained by having to grapple with the convergence-divergence issue on the basis of sequential country-by-country descriptions, and without the benefit of access to strictly comparable measures, Cranet researchers have been able to simultaneously analyze developments across a range of countries in terms of precisely defined HRM practices. Gooderham and Brewster (2003) found evidence of convergence towards the "Americanization" of HRM, though they also noted significant differences between the countries. HRM convergence was explored in detail by Mayrhofer et al. (2011), who looked at the position in Europe over two decades. They found evidence of some clear trends in HRM, in, for example, increasing individualization of HRM, and increased communication within organizations, in a steady rise in contingent pay systems and a centralization of policy-making towards the HRM department and away from line management. They found no evidence of country "recipes" losing their force or countries becoming more alike in their HRM.

In detail, Cranet researchers find that, for example, union membership, employers' recognition of unions, policy determination in industrial relations, and communications between management and employees, showed similar trends, but across-Europe distinctive national patterns of industrial relations remained steady (Gunnigle, Brewster, and Morley 1994; Morley et al. 1996). Similarly, later research (Brewster et al. 2007) also largely rejected the notion that there has been a development from collective towards individual voice mechanisms. It was concluded that collective voice still remains significant in large work organizations.

Larsen and Brewster (2003), examining the decentralization or delegation of HRM responsibilities to the line management over a ten-year period, found that the positions of the countries they examined, relative to one another, did not change. In that sense, they observed no significant convergence.

Nikandrou, Apospori, and Papalexandris (2005) longitudinally examined HRM strategies and practices and the role of HRM within organizations in 18 European countries. Adopting a country-level analysis, they employed cluster analysis to group the countries at both points in time. Two stable major clusters were identified, indicating a systematic North/West–South/East distinction in respect to HRM practices. No signs of convergence between these two clusters were found. However, it was observed that Italy and the former East Germany had moved closer to the North-Western cluster.

Clearly, the findings on convergence from the above studies are complex but largely negative. In that sense, the Cranet research has indicated that what North (1990) refers to as the "rules of the game" are not undergoing dramatic change. This is despite the presence of foreign MNCs in Europe that are sources of local variety, but in fact, largely follow local laws and regulations (Brewster, Wood, and Brookes 2008; Farndale, Poutsma, and Brewster 2008), and despite the latitude that firms have to make strategic decisions.

EVIDENCE FROM CRANET

We offer our account of the findings from Cranet-based research in line with the human resource cycle that applies to employees: covering successively the strategic role of the HRM department and, then, policies that are experienced by employees. We then cover, in turn, recruitment and selection, voice and communication, compensation, training, and tenure. We discuss briefly the Cranet research that has addressed the business outcomes of HRM: productivity and financial performance.

The Strategic Role of the HRM Department in HRM Practices

Looking at the voice and strategy debate from another angle, and using a wider range of countries, Vernon and Brewster (2013) found that in organizations where trade union membership and influence are high, the HRM department is better positioned to play a strategic role. Brewster, Brookes, and Gollan (2015) examined the role of line managers in 11 countries. Organizations in the Nordic economies were most likely to assign HRM responsibilities to the line and LMEs least likely to do so. They also noted that in any economy the least likely to assign HRM responsibilities to the line were larger organizations, unionized organizations, and those with the most strategically positioned HRM departments.

Employing a multi-level analysis, Gooderham et al. (2015) examine the impact of firm and national level characteristics on the location of the primary responsibility for HRM decision-making concerning the following four HRM areas: pay and benefits; recruitment and selection; training and development; and industrial relations. At the national level, they employ Botero et al. (2004) in order to test whether institutional conditions influence the location of HRM decision making. They find support for the notion that, the greater the degree to which the conditions of employment are specified legally, the fewer incentives firms have to develop a specialized HRM function that has decision-making responsibility. Thus, in institutional settings characterized by more rigid employment laws, devolution to line management is greater. This remains the case even when controlling for national culture. However, their multi-level analysis also indicates that firms have a significant degree of latitude to engage in strategic behaviors irrespective of institutional constraints. Thus, they find that the political power of senior HR managers has a unique effect on the ownership of HRM decision-making.

Recruitment and selection

There have been few attempts to use the Cranet data to examine recruitment and performance, and the reason for that may be that the findings are equivocal—pointing to neither uniformity nor diffuse diversity. They show that whilst there are distinctions according to types of comparative capitalisms and the property rights implied under each type, the patterns show as many examples of diversity within a system as between them (Wood et al. 2014). This seems to be an area where context is perhaps less important than managerial agency.

Employer-employee communication

Voice is one of the topics where the comparative capitalisms literature is clearest. It is expected that employees will have least voice in the owner-focused LMEs and more in the stakeholder-focused CMEs. There is now considerable evidence that these predictions are broadly correct (Brewster et al. 2007; Brewster et al. 2014; Brewster, Wood, and Goergen 2015). Brewster et al. (2014) found that, although the picture was complex, both direct and indirect participation varied with setting, being much more likely to occur in CMEs.

Aside from the impact on the firm, the Cranet data have also addressed the debate as to whether other forms of voice "crowd out" formal trade union voice, being used perhaps as a way for management to avoid or bypass the unions. Brewster et al. (2007) found that, in fact, the two systems are much more likely to complement each other than to be substitutes.

Croucher, Gooderham, and Parry (2006) argue that the "Varieties of Capitalism" literature suggests that, as part of a general structural bias towards consensus-building, in particular within organizations (Hall and Soskice 2001), stronger information-sharing is to be expected in CMEs than in LMEs. They examined this thesis by comparing the use of "direct communication," i.e., management information-giving to employees that is not mediated through employee representatives, in the UK, an LME country, and Denmark, a CME country. However, they found no support for national level differences. Instead, they found that despite the marked systemic differences between the two national cases, direct communication has similar antecedents in both countries. In both the UK and Denmark, firms involving their HR managers in strategy development are significantly more likely to have direct communication than those that do not. This finding holds true even when the level of unionization at the firm-level is controlled for. Thus, independent of the unionization factor, a strategic approach to HRM, denoted by the integration of the HRM function into the strategy formulation process, is associated with high levels of direct communication with employees.

Compensation

One early application of comparative institutional theory to compensation is the study of Gooderham, Nordhaug, and Ringdal (1999). After developing a two-fold typology of HRM practices, that distinguished "calculative" and "collaborative" HRM, they categorized six European institutional contexts that they employed to hypothesize differences in the application HRM. While the concept of collaborative HRM captures how employers brief employees on strategy, the concept of calculative HRM encapsulates individualized pay-for-performance (I-PFP) compensation systems. Their findings are particularly clear-cut for the latter. They find that calculative HRM is much more of a feature of the UK than of Germany or Scandinavia. Thus, their findings support the notion that institutional determinants, as indicated by the national embeddedness of firms, have a substantial effect on the application of compensation practices. In a substantial refinement of this analysis, Gooderham et al. (2018) conducted a multi-level analysis of the adoption of I-PFP using data from over 4,000 firms in 26 countries. Using Botero et al.'s (2004) labor regulation approach to conducting cross-national institutional comparisons, as well as a measure of national culture, they find that, at the country level, both culture and the institutional environment explain significant variance in the use of I-PFP. Thus, although they find a high degree of inter-firm variability within countries, country level effects have an important impact on firm behavior. Further, their study indicates that a country's institutions explain unique variance over and above the effect of culture on the use of I-PFP. Moreover, while culture plays some role in determining I-PFP use, this role is entirely mediated via institutional configuration (labor regulation and between-country differences) in the influence of labor unions. As such, their study supports the general approach of Cranet research to focus on comparative institutional theory rather than on culture theory.

Gooderham et al.'s (2015) study also indicates that regardless of country-of-origin, foreign-owned firms, in general, show greater propensity to adopt I-PFP than do domestic firms. Thus, multi-national firms do not necessarily seek to impose home country practices but seem to converge towards a global standard. These findings are in line with the Le et al. (2013) study, which shows that use of management incentives is higher in MNCs than in domestic firms and that the gap between MNCs and domestic firms is lower in the MNCs than in other types of market economy.

Cranet scholars have also studied financial participation, including share schemes and profit sharing. One of the world's leading experts on financial participation, Erik Poutsma, with colleagues (Poutsma, Ligthart, and Schouteten 2005), found that what they called "Anglo-Saxonization" had a significant effect on the likelihood of share schemes and profit sharing, both those aimed just at management and the broad-based schemes, and that this applied both to the LME economies and to the influence of U.S. MNEs within European economies. Kalmi, Pendleton, and Poutsma (2012) used the Cranet data to explore financial participation, and variable pay, in 13 European countries, and found a complex picture. They found that team-based variable pay is most common in centralized pay regimes, and employee share ownership most common in decentralized regimes. Their decentralized regimes are mostly LMEs and the centralized ones CMEs, but this is not consistently the case. Kabst, Matiaske, and Schmelter (2006, 577) examined the UK, France, and Germany and similarly found that "the institutional environment in which the organization is situated affects the occurrence and eligibility of financial participations schemes." Croucher et al. (2010) had similar findings, noting also that collective employee voice (see below) had no impact, but that calculative HRM strategies were significant. In line with Gooderham et al. (2015), Poutsma, Ligthart, and Schouteten (2005) too observe considerable diversity at the within-country level.

Training

Training is more likely to occur in CMEs, according to the literature on comparative capitalisms. With lower turnover, less downsizing, and longer tenure, firms are more likely to invest in developing their employees; those trained employees are more likely to stay with the organization rather than take that investment to competitors. In fact, although these categorizations are broadly correct, and analyses by organizational size or sector had little explanatory power, the Cranet data shows a need for a more nuanced picture, with significant variation within the CME group (Goergen et al. 2012).

Tenure

Tenure will be longer in the CMEs than in the more transactional LMEs. In LMEs, the opportunities for employee dismissal for economic reasons are relatively unconstrained, whilst in CMEs there is a tradition of long-term labor contracts and substantially greater security against arbitrary lay-offs. This was tested by Croucher et al. (2012). They used Amable's (2003) more differentiated view of distinctions within the CME group, separating out the Nordic group, and found that exit, forced or voluntary, is more common in the LME countries and least common in the CMEs, with the Nordic group somewhere between the two. Similarly, Goergen, Brewster, and Wood (2013) found that downsizing was not explained by differences in varieties of capitalism, nor by legal origins, but was correlated with differences in political systems, being less common in those countries with proportional representation.

Looking across these findings, it seems that some HRM practices, such as representative employee voice, compensation and tenure are more impacted by context than others, where managements may have greater agency.

HRM outcomes. What about the outcomes of HRM policies and practices? A substantial proportion of the most highly cited empirical studies of HRM have as their primary focus the relationship between HRM and organizational performance, not least productivity and financial performance (Jackson, Schuler, and Jiang 2014). Cranet research contains several examples of this relationship but differs by studying financial performance outcomes across a variety of contexts, not least national context.

Productivity and financial performance

A driving force behind the emergence of the narrow strategic view of HRM was the belief that HRM practices should serve the owners of the business and enhance organizational performance, not least in a short-term financial sense (Schuler and Jackson 2005). Paralleling this, numerous theorists have argued that the human resources of the firm are potentially a powerful source of sustainable competitive advantage, and have sought to demonstrate that there is a positive relationship between HRM and firm performance (Appelbaum, Berg, and Kalleberg 2000; Guest 1997; Huselid 1995; Paauwe, Guest, and Wright 2013).

Stavrou-Costea (2005) studied HRM challenges in southern EU countries and their effect on organizational performance. On the basis of the existing literature, she identified a number of basic challenges that involved training and development, efficiency and flexibility, and employee relations. She found that these were related to firm productivity in most of southern EU.

Apospori et al. (2008) also included southern Europe in their analysis of the firm-level impact of strategic HRM practices on organizational performance. They clustered these countries and compared them to a cluster of northern European countries. Adopting a contingency approach, they developed a structural model that considered direct and indirect influences of market growth, business strategy formalization, and HRM centrality and practices on organizational performance in Europe. Their study revealed differences between northern and southern Europe. Clear differences appeared between the two clusters in the HRM policies and practices correlated with higher performance, thus indicating that the link between HRM and performance may be different in various geographies. Apospori et al. (2008, 1202) concluded that "[t]reating various European countries together may disguise interesting differences; based on this assumption the present research studied the two major groups of countries identified in cluster analysis. However, further division of the two clusters into sub-clusters would give us more refined estimates of the found impacts and reveal some more interesting differences."

In other words, they indicate the need to include country, rather than clusters of countries, in future analyses. This is precisely the strategy adopted by Gooderham, Parry, and Ringdal (2008) and Rizov and Croucher (2008). Gooderham et al. (2008) examined the extent to which HRM practices have a significant impact on whether gross revenue over the past three years has been well in excess of costs or not. Deploying factor analysis on as many as 60 HRM practices contained in the Cranet data set, they identify six bundles of calculative practices, six bundles of collaborative practices, and three "intermediary" bundles. Their findings both support and cast some doubt on the value of HRM for firm performance in the context of Europe in that their findings are different in regard to calculative and collaborative HRM. While they found that calculative and intermediary HRM bundles, with exceptions, generally have some impact on the performance of European firms, collaborative HRM bundles do not. They found no support for the notion that these HRM bundles would be contingent on an interaction with a range of external and internal factors. They observed that, for European firms, the country of location is a relatively important source of variation in performance. This was ascribed to differences in national economic cycles, but they also speculated that country of location may reflect the efficacy of national business systems in delivering profits for owners. The authors argued that future studies should be designed to differentiate between cyclical economic conditions and long-term institutional conditions.

Rizov and Croucher's (2008) study of HRM and performance in Europe also adopts the calculative/collaborative HRM dichotomy. However, unlike Gooderham et al., who differentiated between various bundles of calculative and collaborative HRM, Rizov and Croucher used only two composite HRM measures. Another difference is that Rizov and Croucher's measure of self-reported measure of firm performance is significantly broader, being a composite index comprised of five partial measures: service quality, level of productivity, profitability, product to market time, and rate of innovation. However, despite these differences, when Rizov and Croucher tested the relationship between HRM practices and firm performance, they also found, like Gooderham et al. (2008), that while calculative HRM has a positive impact on performance, collaborative HRM has no effect.

Rizov and Croucher then inter-acted the two HRM variables with country dummies. This had noticeable consequences. First, while the effect of collaborative HRM on performance remained non-significant, the effect of calculative HRM was now also non-significant. Overall, their analysis indicated virtually no significant country-calculative HRM interaction effects on performance. Instead, their analysis indicated positive interaction effects of collaborative practices for several CME countries including France, Germany, and Denmark, though no such effects for several other CME countries such as Belgium, Austria, and Norway. This assortment of findings was also the case when Rizov and Croucher tested for absenteeism and employee turnover rather than performance. Nevertheless, they concluded that the evidence suggests that collaborative HRM is more likely than calculative HRM to enhance firm performance when one takes into account the institutional setting. In short, firms located in high trust CME countries are more conducive to generating performance effects from collaborative HRM than LME countries such as the UK. On this basis, Rizov and Croucher (2008:18) argued that their findings "demonstrate that the CME model is superior in supporting productive efficiency at the organizational level."

Taken together, and allowing for differences in operationalizations of firm performance, these studies indicate that the effect of HRM on firm performance is somewhat limited. This is particularly the case when firm performance is defined in terms of purely financial performance. Furthermore, both studies indicate that country of location is a factor that influences firm performance. Whereas Rizov and Croucher ascribe this to institutional setting and, thus, argue for the superiority of the CME institutional setting, Gooderham et al. (2008) point to an alternative possibility, that of variation in national economic cycles. This would account for the variation Rizov and Croucher observed between CME countries in relation to collaborative HRM. However, Gooderham et al. also speculate that country of location may reflect the efficacy of national business systems.

PROPOSALS

We have argued that HRM research needs to take more account of context, perhaps particularly using the neo-institutional lens. Moreover, these differences are not going away: there is little sign of convergence. We have also shown that the researchers in the Cranet network have made a significant contribution already to that research drive. Where do the theories and the evidence take us for the immediate future? Each of the areas studied so far by the network leaves considerable room for development. A weakness of the Cranet data is that it can show differences in terms of numbers and percentage but not in terms of quality. Thus, we can measure the number of organizations using particular recruitment patterns or dealing with trade unions, but we cannot tell from this evidence how well they do that. There is a need for more detailed comparative research on all these topics.

We close this article by suggesting four areas of potential research that might be said to arise directly from the evidence we have outlined. These are as follows: expanding the research beyond Europe; clarifying the role of managerial autonomy; the role of MNEs in bringing in new HRM practices; the impact of time, in particular the effects of factors such as economic crisis on a country's HRM practices years later and the extent of convergence or divergence.

Expanding the research beyond Europe is obviously needed given the Euro-centric nature of the research noted. It is becoming more of a possibility as Cranet collects solid data from North and South America and Asia. Although it is the focus of this issue, Cranet, of course, is not the only source of comparable data on HRM, and we look forward to other evidence being developed. There are ever greater numbers of qualified researchers from almost every country in the world, and the research into emerging countries and their multinational corporations is growing apace and showing the importance of context and of not assuming that things will work the same way in different contexts.

Clarifying the role of managerial autonomy is, in a sense, a counter-balance to the insistence of the neo-institutional literature that managers are not free to do as they wish but rather are tightly constrained in their actions—at least, if they wish to be legitimate and effective. In fact, literature shows that there is room for managerial agency: We just do not know how much room. To what extent can managers act outside the cultural and institutional norms and still be effective? In some contexts, institutions may be weak and not be deeply embedded in the fabric of the country. For example, in some developing counties the power of certain families, tradition, and/or corruption may be more powerful than government enforcement. We need more research that examines the role of managerial agency and the balance between that and the institutional constraint.

The role of MNEs follows a similar line of argument. How much freedom do they have to act differently from other organizations in the host countries? There has been much debate, and there is still much to learn. The Cranet evidence (Brewster, Wood, and Brookes 2008; Farndale, Poutsma, and Brewster 2008; Fenton-O'Creevy, Gooderham, and Nordhaug 2008; Gooderham, Nordhaug, and Ringdal 2006), unlike many other contributions, is able to compare MNEs and indigenous firms directly, and that evidence seems to show that MNEs are different from indigenous firms, but not that different. Basically, they have to deal with the same education system, labor market, and employment and fiscal laws as all other organizations. In the LMEs, multinational firms follow LME practices; in CMEs they are more likely to follow CME practices. But they are innovators in each society, and they do some things differently; we need greater understanding of what these things are, what enables and constrains them, and how these might be explained.

The impact of time has been largely ignored in HRM research (Hippler, Brewster, and Haslberger 2015; Sonnentag 2012) but is clearly critical. The discussion of convergence above is a case in point. Unless we can measure changes in HRM over time, and ensure that we are comparing data collected at the same time point, we will not be able to understand the impact of context fully when we do international comparisons. There is an urgent need for more longitudinal analyses.

REFERENCES

Amable, B. 2003. *The Diversity of Modern Capitalism*. Oxford: Oxford University Press.

Apospori, E., I. Nikandrou, C. Brewster, and N. Papalexandris. 2008. "HRM and Organizational Performance in Northern and Southern Europe." *The International Journal of Human Resource Management* 19 (7):1187–207. doi:10.1080/09585190802109788.

Appelbaum, E., P. Berg, and A. Kalleberg. 2000. *Manufacturing Advantage: Why High-Performance Work Systems Pay Off*. Ithaca, NY: Cornell University Press.

Avloniti, A., and F. Filippaios. 2014. "Evaluating the Effects of Cultural Difference on Corporate Performance: A Meta-Analysis of the Existing Literature." *International Business Review* 23 (3):660–74. doi:10.1016/j.ibusrev.2013.11.007.

Beer, M., B. Spector, R. Lawrence, M. D. Quinn, and E. Walton. 1984. *Managing Human Assets: The Ground Breaking Harvard Business School Program*. New York, NY: Free Press.

Botero, J. C., S. Djankov, R. L. Porta, F. Lopez-de-Silanes, and A. Shleifer. 2004. "The Regulation of Labor." *The Quarterly Journal of Economics* 119 (4):1339–182. doi:10.1162/0033553042476215.

Brewster, C. and W, Mayrhofer (Eds). 2012. *A Handbook of Research into Comparative Human Resource Management Practice*. Cheltenham, UK: Edward Elgar.

Brewster, C., M. Brookes, and P. J. Gollan. 2015. "The Institutional Antecedents of the Assignment of HRM Responsibilities to Line Managers." *Human Resource Management* 54 (4):577–97. doi:10.1002/hrm.21632.

Brewster, C., M. Brookes., P. Johnson, and G. Wood. 2014. "Direct Involvement, Partnership and Setting: A Study in Bounded Diversity." *The International Journal of Human Resource Management* 25 (6):795–809. doi:10.1080/09585192.2013.776615.

Brewster, C., R. Croucher, G. Wood, and M. Brookes. 2007. "Collective and Individual Voice: Convergence in Europe?" *The International Journal of Human Resource Management* 18 (7):1246–62. doi:10.1080/09585190701393582.

Brewster, C., G. Wood, and M. Brookes. 2008. "Similarity, Isomorphism and Duality? Recent Survey Evidence on the HRM Policies of MNCs." *British Journal of Management* 19 (4):320–42. doi:10.1111/j.1467-8551.2007.00546.x.

Brewster, C., G. Wood, and M. Goergen. 2015. "Institutions, Unionization and Voice: The Relative Impact of Context and Actors on Firm Level Practice." *Economic and Industrial Democracy* 36 (2):195–214. doi:10.1177/0143831X13501004.

Brewster, C., G. Wood, C. Croucher, and M. Brookes. 2007. "Are Works Councils and Joint Consultative Committees a Threat to Trade Unions? a Comparative Analysis." *Economic and Industrial Democracy* 28 (1): 49–81. doi:10.1177/0143831X07073027.

Croucher, R., M. Brookes, G. Wood, and C. Brewster. 2010. "Context, Strategy and Financial Participation: A Comparative Analysis." *Human Relations* 63 (6):835–55. doi:10.1177/0018726709343654.

Croucher, R., P. N. Gooderham, and E. Parry. 2006. "The Influence of Direct Communication in British and Danish Firms: Country, 'Strategic HRM' or Unionization?" *European Journal of Industrial Relations* 12 (3):267–86. doi: 10.1177/0959680106068913.

Croucher, R., G. Wood, C. Brewster, and M. Brookes. 2012. "Employee Turnover, HRM and Institutional Contexts." *Economic and Industrial Democracy* 33 (4):605–20. doi:10.1177/0143831X11424768.

Delbridge, R., M. Hauptmeier, and S. Sengupta. 2011. "Beyond the Enterprise: Broadening the Horizons of International HRM." *Human Relations* 64 (4):483–505. doi:10.1177/0018726710396388.

DiMaggio, P. J., and W. W. Powell. 1983. "The Iron Cage Revisited: Institutional Isomorphism and Collective Rationality in Organizational Fields." *American Sociological Review* 48 (2):147–60. doi:10.2307/2095101.

Drori, G. S., J. W. Meyer, and H. Hwang. 2006. "Introduction." In *Globalization and Organization: World Society and Organizational Change*, edited by G. S. Drori, J. W. Meyer and H. Hwang, 1–22. Oxford University Press.

Farndale, E., E. Poutsma, and C. Brewster. 2008. "Coordinated versus Liberal Market HRM: The Impact of Institutionalization on Multinational Firms." *The International Journal of Human Resource Management* 19 (11): 2004–23. doi:10.1080/09585190802404247.

Fenton-O'Creevy, M., P. N. Gooderham, and O. Nordhaug. 2008. "HRM in US Subsidiaries in Europe and Australia: Centralization or Autonomy?" *Journal of International Business Studies* 39 (1):151–66. doi:10.1057/palgrave.jibs.8400313.

Fombrun, C. J., N. M. Tichy, and M. A. Devanna. 1984. *Strategic Human Resource Management*. New York, NY: John Wiley and Sons, Inc.

Goergen, M., C. Brewster, G. T. Wood, and A. Wilkinson. 2012. "Varieties of Capitalism and Investments in Human Capital." *Industrial Relations: A Journal of Economy and Society* 51 (2):501–27. doi:10.1111/j.1468-232X.2012.00688.x.

Goergen, M., C. Brewster, and G. T. Wood. 2013. "The Effects of the National Setting on Employment Practice: The Case of Downsizing." *International Business Review* 22 (6):1051–67. doi:10.1016/j.ibusrev.2013.02.001.

Gooderham, P. N., and C. Brewster. 2003. "Convergence, Stasis or Divergence? Personnel Management in Europe." *Scandinavian Journal of Business Research* 17 (1):7–18.

Gooderham, P. N., M. Fenton-O'Creevy, R. Croucher, and M. Brookes. 2018. "A Multi-Level Analysis of the Use of Individual Pay-for-Performance Systems." *Journal of Management* 44 (4):1479–504. doi:10.1177/0149206315610634.

Gooderham, P., M. J. Morley, E. Parry, and E. E. Stavrou. 2015. "National and Firm Level Drivers of the Devolution of HRM Decision Making to Line Managers." *Journal of International Business Studies* 46 (6): 715–23. doi:10.1057/jibs.2015.5.

Gooderham, P. N., O. Nordhaug, and K. Ringdal. 1999. "Institutional Determinants of Organizational Practices: Human Resource Management in European Firms." *Administrative Science Quarterly* 44 (3):507–31. doi:10.2307/2666960.

Gooderham, P. N., O. Nordhaug, and K. Ringdal. 2006. "National Embeddedness and HRM Practices in US Subsidiaries in Europe and Australia." *Human Relations* 59 (11):1491–513. doi:10.1177/0018726706072843.

Gooderham, P. N., E. Parry, and K. Ringdal. 2008. "The Impact of Bundles of Strategic Human Resource Management Practices on the Performance of European Firms." *The International Journal of Human Resource Management* 19 (11):2041–56. doi:10.1080/09585190802404296.

Gospel, H. F., and A. Pendleton. 2005. "Corporate Governance and Labor Management: An International Comparison." In *Corporate Governance and Labor Management: An International Comparison*, edited by . H.F Gospel and A. Pendelton, 1–32. Oxford, UK: Oxford University Press.

Guest, D. 1990. "Human Resource Management and the American Dream." *Journal of Management Studies* 27 (4): 377–97. doi:10.1111/j.1467-6486.1990.tb00253.x.

Guest, D. E. 1997. "Human Resource Management and Performance: A Review and Research Agenda." *The International Journal of Human Resource Management* 8 (3):263–76. doi:10.1080/095851997341630.

Gunnigle, P., C. Brewster, and M. J. Morley. 1994. "Continuity and Change in European Industrial Relations, Evidence from a 14 Country Study." *Personnel Review* 23 (3):4–20. doi:10.1108/00483489410064531.

Hall, P. and D. Soskice (Eds.). 2001. *Varieties of Capitalism: The Institutional Basis of Competitive Advantage*. Oxford, UK: Oxford University Press.

Hippler, T., C. Brewster, and A. Haslberger. 2015. "The Elephant in the Room: The Role of Time in Expatriate Adjustment." *The International Journal of Human Resource Management* 26 (15):1920–35. doi:10.1080/09585192.2015.1041762.

Hoffmann, A. 1999. "Institutional Evolution and Change: Environmentalism and the U.S. Chemical Industry." *Academy of Management Journal* 42 (4):351–71. doi:10.5465/257008.

Huselid, M. A. 1995. "The Impact of Human Resource Management Practices on Turnover, Productivity and Corporate Financial Performance." *Academy of Management Journal* 38 (3):635–70. doi:10.2307/256741.

Jackson, G., and R. Deeg. 2008. "Comparing Capitalisms: Understanding Institutional Diversity and Its Implications for International Business." *Journal of International Business Studies* 39 (4):540–61. doi:10.1057/palgrave.jibs.8400375.

Jackson, S. E., R. S. Schuler, and K. Jiang. 2014. "An Aspirational Framework for Strategic Human Resource Management." *Academy of Management Annals* 8 (1):1–56. doi:10.5465/19416520.2014.872335.

Kabst, R., W. Matiaske, and A. Schmelter. 2006. "Financial Participation in British, French and German Organizations: A Neo-Institutionalist Perspective." *Economic and Industrial Democracy* 27 (4):565–85. doi:10.1177/0143831X06068994.

Kalmi, P., A. Pendleton, and E. Poutsma. 2012. "Bargaining Regimes, Variable Pay and Financial Participation: Some Survey Evidence on Pay Determination." *The International Journal of Human Resource Management* 23 (8):1643–59. doi:10.1080/09585192.2012.661993.

Kaufman, B. E. 2015. "Evolution of Strategic HRM as Seen through Two Founding Books: A 30th Anniversary Perspective on Development of the Field." *Human Resource Management* 54 (3):389–407. doi:10.1002/hrm.21720.

Kidger, P. J. 1991. "The Emergence of International Human Resource Management." *The International Journal of Human Resource Management* 2 (2):149–53. doi:10.1080/09585198100000003.

Larsen, H. H., and C. Brewster. 2003. "Line Management Responsibility for HRM: What Is Happening in Europe?" *Employee Relations* 25 (3):228–44. doi:10.1108/01425450310475838.

Le, Hang, Chris Brewster, Mehmet Demirbag, and Geoffrey Wood. 2013. "Management Compensation in MNCs and Domestic Firms." *Management International Review* 53 (5):741–62. doi:10.1007/s11575-013-0175-2.

Legge, K. 1995. *Human Resource Management: Rhetorics and Realities*. Basingstoke, UK: MacMillan Business.

Mayrhofer, W., C. Brewster, M. Morley, and J. Ledolter. 2011. "Hearing a Different Drummer? Evidence of Convergence in European HRM." *Human Resource Management Review* 21 (1):50–67. doi:10.1016/j.hrmr.2010.09.011.

Meyer, K. E., R. Mudambi, and R. Narula. 2011. "Multinational Enterprises and Local Contexts: The Opportunities and Challenges of Multiple Embeddedness." *Journal of Management Studies* 48 (2):235–52. doi:10.1111/j.1467-6486.2010.00968.x.

Meyer, J. W., and B. Rowan. 1983. "Institutionalized Organizations: Formal Structure as Myth and Ceremony." In *Organizational Environments Ritual and Rationality*, edited by W. Meyer, B. Rowan and T. E. Deal, 21–44. Beverly Hills, CA: Sage Publications.

Morley, M.,. C. Brewster, P. Gunnigle, and W. Mayrhofer. 1996. "Evaluating Change in European Industrial Relations: Research Evidence on Trends at Organizational Level." *The International Journal of Human Resource Management* 7 (3):640–56. doi:10.1080/09585199600000148.

Nikandrou, F., E. Apospori, and N. Papalexandris. 2005. "Changes in HRM in Europe: A Longitudinal Comparative Study among 18." *Journal of European Industrial Training* 29 (7):541–60. doi:10.1108/03090590510621045.

Nikandrou, I., E. Apospori., L. Panayotopoulou, E. Stavrou, and N. Papalexandris. 2008. "Training and Firm Performance in Europe: The Impact of National and Organizational Characteristics." *The International Journal of Human Resource Management* 19 (11):2057–78. doi:10.1080/09585190802404304.

North, D. C. 1990. *Institutions, Institutional Change and Economic Performance*. Cambridge, UK: Cambridge University Press.

Oliver, C. 1991. "Strategic Responses to Institutional Processes." *Academy of Management Review* 16 (1):145–79. doi:10.5465/amr.1991.4279002.

Paauwe, J., D. Guest and P. M. Wright (Eds.). 2013. *HRM and Performance: Achievements and Challenges*. Chichester, UK: John Wiley and Sons.

Pagano, M., and P. Volpin. 2005. "The Political Economy of Corporate Governance." *American Economic Review* 95 (4):1005–30. doi:10.1257/0002828054825646.

Poutsma, Erik, Paul E. M. Ligthart, and Roel Schouteten. 2005. "Employee Share Ownership in Europe: The Influence of US Multinationals." *Management Revu* 16 (1):99–122. doi:10.5771/0935-9915-2005-1-99.

Powell, W., and P. DiMaggio. 1991. *The New Institutionalism in Organizational Analysis*. Chicago, IL: University of Chicago Press.

Rizov, M., and R. Croucher. 2008. "Human Resource Management and Performance in European Firms." *Cambridge Journal of Economics* 33 (2):253–72. doi:10.1093/cje/ben037.

Roe, M. 2003. *Political Determinants of Corporate Governance*. Oxford, UK: Oxford University Press.

Rynes, S. L., K. G. Brown, and A. E. Colbert. 2002. "Seven Common Misconceptions about Human Resource Practices: Research Findings versus Practitioner Beliefs." *Academy of Management Perspectives* 16 (3):92–102. doi:10.5465/ame.2002.8540341.

Rynes, S. L., T. L. Giluk, and K. G. Brown. 2007. "The Very Separate Worlds of Academic and Practitioner Periodicals in Human Resource Management: Implications for Evidence-Based Management." *Academy of Management Journal* 50 (5):987–1008. doi:10.5465/amj.2007.27151939.

Schuler, R. S., and S. Jackson. 2005. "A Quarter-Century Review of Human Resource Management in the U.S.: The Growth in Importance of the International Perspective." *Management Revu* 16 (1):11–35. doi:10.5771/0935-9915-2005-1-11.

Scott, W. R. 1991. "Unpacking Institutional Arguments." In *The New Institutionalism in Organizational Analysis*, edited by W. Powell and P. DiMaggio, 164–82. Chicago, UK: University of Chicago Press.

Scott, W. R. 1995. *Institutions and Organizations: Ideas and Interests*. Thousand Oaks, CA: Sage.

Sonnentag, S. 2012. "Time in Organizational Research: Catching up on a Long Neglected Topic in Order to Improve Theory." *Organizational Psychology Review* 2 (4):361–8. doi:10.1177/2041386612442079.

Sparrow, P., and M. Hiltrop. 1994. *European Human Resource Management in Transition*. New York, NY: Prentice Hall.

Stavrou-Costea, E. 2005. "The Challenges of Human Resource Management towards Organizational Effectiveness: A Comparative Study in Southern EU." *Journal of European Industrial Training* 29 (2–3):112–34.

Thelen, K. 2014. *Varieties of Liberalization and the New Politics of Social Solidarity*. Cambridge, UK: Cambridge University Press.

Vaiman, V., and C. Brewster. 2015. "Comparative Explanations of Comparative HRM: Assessing Cultural and Institutional Theories." *The International Journal of Human Resource Management* 26 (2):151–64. doi:10.1080/09585192.2014.937969.

Vernon, G., and C. Brewster. 2013. "Structural Spoilers or Structural Supports? Unionism and the Strategic Integration of HR Functions." *The International Journal of Human Resource Management* 24 (6):1113–30. doi:10.1080/09585192.2012.703416.

Walker, J. T., C. Brewster, and G. Wood. 2014. "Diversity between and within Varieties of Capitalism: Transnational Survey Evidence." *Industrial and Corporate Change* 23 (2):493–533. doi:10.1093/icc/dtt014.

Walton, R. E. 1985. "Toward a Strategy of Eliciting Employee Commitment Based on Policies of Mutuality." In *Human Resource Management: Trends and Challenges*, edited by R. E. Walton and P. R. Lawrence, 35–65. Boston, MA: Harvard Business School Press.

Wangrow, David B., Donald J. Schepker, and Vincent L. Barker. 2015. "Managerial Discretion: An Empirical Review and Focus on Future Research Directions." *Journal of Management* 41 (1):99–135. doi:10.1177/0149206314554214.

Whitley, R. 1999. *Divergent Capitalisms: The Social Structuring and Change of Business Systems*. Oxford, UK: Oxford University Press.

Wood, G. T., C. Brewster, M. Demirbag, and M. Brookes. 2014. "Understanding Contextual Differences in Employee Resourcing" In *Human Resource Management and the Institutional Perspective*, edited by G. T. Wood, C. Brewster and M. Brookes, 25–38. London, UK: Routledge

Wright, P., and L. Nishii. 2013. "Strategic HRM and Organizational Behavior: Integrating Multiple Levels of Analysis." In *HRM and Performance: Building the Evidence Base*, edited by D. E. Guest, J. Paauwe and P. M. Wright, 97–110. San Francisco, CA: John Wiley and Sons.

A Comparative Study of Trade Union Influence over HRM Practices in Spanish and Brazilian Firms: The Role of Industrial Relations Systems and Their Historical Evolution

Wilson Aparecido Costa de Amorim, Andre Luiz Fischer and Jordi Trullen

Abstract: This study explores trade union influence over human resource management (HRM) practices in Spanish and Brazilian organizations using the Cranet 2014 dataset. While some of the existing data suggest that trade unions may hold little power within surveyed organizations, we offer additional evidence contradicting this. Trade unions' influence is better understood when taking into account the industrial relations systems of Spain and Brazil, as well as their historical evolution. Understanding such evolution helps us account for similarities and differences observed in the way trade unions influence HRM in these two countries.

INTRODUCTION

The notion of Human Resource Management (HRM), with its origin in American business schools, has quickly spread around the world, despite some of its core assumptions being diverse from prevalent norms in other countries (Brewster 2007). One particular area of contention in that respect refers to the role that trade unions play in different countries and their degree of influence on HRM policies. While HRM assumes that employers have a great deal of discretion in dealing with employees, the strong influence of trade unions in some countries significantly challenges this assumption. There is, however, enough evidence to argue that directional convergence (Mayrhofer and Brewster 2005) is taking place in HRM and that anti-trade union attitudes and a progressive individualization of employer–employee relationships are also spreading to other regions (Mitchell and Fetter 2003; Storey and Bacon 1993).

The present research focuses on two of those regions, Europe and Latin America, by exploring the role played by trade unions in Spanish and Brazilian organizations. While both Spain and Brazil have long traditions of collectivism, which provide trade unions with social legitimacy and power (Lucena and Covarrubia 2006; Morley et al. 1996), the introduction of innovative work systems as a result of the entry of foreign multinationals, as well as the internationalization of formerly state-owned companies (Anner and Cândia Veiga 2013; Ferner and Quintanilla 2002), has also contributed to the development of anti-union attitudes and perceptions in these countries. It is, therefore, interesting to check the extent to which trade unions' influence remains strong or, on the contrary, has become weaker over time.

In the specific case of these two countries, a comparative study is appropriate. Latin America is still a little-explored subject in organizational studies, and even more particularly when it comes to HRM. Within this region—and as its largest country and economy—Brazil has been an increasingly important participant in the world's capital, technology, and labor flows. Nonetheless, it remains uncharted territory for this field of research (Elvira and Davila 2005; Souza et al. 2014). As for Spain, although a member of the European Union, it shares several historic and cultural ties with Latin America (Pla-Barber and Camps 2012). In addition, Spanish companies have made heavy investments in Latin America over the last few decades. In Brazil, most of these investments were made in the banking, telecommunications, energy, and infrastructure sectors (ECLAC 2016). This study does not focus specifically on HRM methods employed by Spanish companies operating in Brazil, or vice versa, but the study may provide a better understanding of the particular labor relations issues faced by these companies.

Using data from Cranet, an international research network dedicated to analyzing HRM developments in public- and private-sector organizations with more than 100 employees in different countries (Brewster, Mayrhofer, and Morley 2004), we analyze the influence that trade unions hold within surveyed organizations in these two countries today. In so doing, we find paradoxical results. On the one hand, surveyed managers rate as low the level of influence that trade unions exert in their organizations. We also observe a clear preference of both management and employees for direct and individualized communication. In addition, low unionization rates are characteristic of both countries. On the other hand, there is also additional evidence, both obtained from Cranet and from other sources (DIEESE 2013; Ministerio de Empleo y Seguridad Social 2013), that trade unions have grown somewhat stronger in the past few years. For example, this can be observed in the increased number of strikes initiated by trade unions both in Brazil (Amorim and Santos 2012) and Spain (Sanz de Miguel 2012). In addition, our data indicate that managers continue to recognize trade unions as crucial stakeholders in organizations, and still significantly responsible for negotiating employees' basic salaries, mainly those of clerical and manual workers.

To better understand these findings, we interpret them in the light of the industrial relations systems of Spain and Brazil. We also show how diverse paths in the historical development of the trade union movement in these countries can help us make sense of differences and similarities between the two countries reported in the Cranet data. Examining these different historical paths proves important because of their influence on the structures and rules governing industrial relations in both countries. Such accounts help understand the path dependence nature that follows the formation of these systems, as well as their influence on current HRM practices (Hall and Soskice 2003; Nelson 1996).

The article is organized as follows. First, we provide an overview of the Spanish and Brazilian industrial relations contexts and compare them to each other. Second, we analyze and compare Cranet data collected in 2014, on the influence that trade unions hold on HRM both in Spanish and Brazilian organizations. We conclude by discussing how such data can be better understood in light of both countries' industrial relations systems and their historical contexts.

INDUSTRIAL RELATIONS CONTEXTS IN SPAIN AND BRAZIL

In this section, we offer an overview of the industrial relations systems in Spain and Brazil. We compare both systems on a set of dimensions that include unions' structure and density, source of funding, collective bargaining processes, as well as union activity and influence. Table 1 below summarizes our main findings.

Organizational Structure and Union Density

Spain. According to the Workers' Statute of 1980 and the Law on Trade Union Freedom of 1985, there is a dualistic system of employee participation by trade union bodies at the enterprise and supra-enterprise levels and by works councils elected by workforces in firms with more than 50 employees. Smaller firms elect employee delegates (Köhler and Calleja Jiménez 2013). Works councils do not formally depend on union involvement, but in practice unions play a central role, since the majority of elected representatives are nominated by the unions (Fulton 2013). The origin of works councils can be traced back to the Law of Collective Bargaining, passed in 1958 under the Franco regime. This law allowed workers to negotiate general wage agreements at the firm level for the first time (Pérez-Yruela 1997). For that purpose, workers created shop-floor committees (*comités de base*), which were dissolved after each negotiating exercise. Even though their existence was not legally recognized at the time, authorities started allowing shop-floor committees to organize on a temporary basis, in order to facilitate collective bargaining.

More than two decades later, the Workers' Statute of 1980 was adopted, forcing companies with 50 or more employees to legally recognize shop-floor committees. The workers' committees are entitled to discuss several matters concerning the hiring of employees, and have become representative bodies, operating under the influence of trade unions. More recently, another important step towards strengthening the role of Spanish trade unions was the creation of the European Works Councils Directive in 1994 (European Parliament and of the Council 2009). Valid in all member states of the European Union, this Directive has ensured workers of multinational companies the right to information of interest in employment in two or more countries in which the companies operate (Belizón et al. 2014).

TABLE 1
Industrial Relations Systems Features in Spain and Brazil

Aspects	Spain	Brazil
Organizational Structure and Union Density	Formal structure is sectorial and vertical: unions, federations and confederations. Union does not have monopoly of representation in its territorial base (federations and confederations have no territorial monopoly). Dual system of representation: a) labor unions by company and supra-enterprise level; b) workers' councils at companies. Union Density: 18.9% of workers	Formal structure is sectorial and vertical: unions, federations and confederations Union has monopoly of representation in its territorial base (federations and confederations have no territorial monopoly). Single system of representation through unions at supra-enterprise level: the labor law does not support works councils at companies. Union Density: approximately 17% of workers
Sources of Funding	Public funds and monthly fees of union workers. Public financial aid is based on the number of delegates obtained in elections.	Public funds (formed from an annual tax, equivalent to a workday of any formally employed Brazilian person, unionized or nonunionized) and monthly fees of union workers. Public financial aid is transferred to legal unions according the number of employees represented (unionized or nonunionized).
Collective Bargaining	Nationwide, regional or sectorial agreements linked to firm level agreements. Works councils are also involved in collective bargaining, and monitor collective agreement compliance at the firm level.	By law, collective agreements cover all industry workers. Common collective agreements are sectoral and regional; nationwide sectoral agreements are rare. Agreements at firm level occur in small numbers and usually address specific issues.
Union Activity and Influence	Trade unions are called regularly to discuss major national labor relations issues with government and trade associations. Strike activity is significant. In the period 2012–2013 there was an increase of strikes. 60% of the strikes were initiated by works councils at the company level.	Trade unions are called regularly to discuss major national labor relations issues with government and trade associations. In the recent period (2003–2013) there was an increase of strikes. Strikes involved unionized and nonunionized workers.

The two largest and most important trade union associations in Spain are *Comisiones Obreras* (CCOO) and *Unión General de Trabajadores* (UGT). They both have similar membership levels (approx. 1,100,000 members each) (CCOO 2013; Sanz de Miguel 2012). Both UGT and CCOO have a parent organization structured around industries (e.g., metalworking, public services, communications and transport, and financial services) and different Spanish regions. Following a number of mergers, the CCOO has 11 federations affiliated with it and the UGT has ten. According to the CCOO 2012 annual report (CCOO 2013), both CCOO and UGT have similar levels of support in work council elections, with 33.54 percent of votes for CCOO and 31.30 percent for UGT. CCOO and UGT alone take almost two thirds of the votes and three quarters of the representatives in works council elections. Due to the large number of votes these unions obtain in work council elections, both CCOO and UGT have the status of "most representative" (Jódar et al. 2012). This is important because only trade union associations granted "most representative" status at the national and regional levels, and the representative trade unions at the sectoral level are entitled to negotiate sectoral collective agreements or participate in tripartite bodies (Sanz de Miguel 2014).

Union density–the ratio of salary earners that are trade union members divided by the total number of salary earners—was only 17.2 percent in Spain in 2013 (Visser, Hayter, and Gammarano 2015). However, the fact that work council seats are predominantly occupied by union members provides unions with more influence than the one officially recognized by affiliation rates.

Brazil. The formalization of labor relations took place in Brazil in the 1930s (Barbosa 2007). Getúlio Vargas, who ruled as a dictator from 1930 to 1945, established the Brazilian labor laws and the main institutions of the industrial relations system that largely persist to this day. The Consolidation of Labor Laws (CLT), inspired by the Charter of Labor of 1927 (*Carta del Lavoro*) of the Italian fascist regime, emerged in 1943 and strongly tied employer associations (in Brazil called "employers union") and employees unions to the State. In this spirit, trade associations and employee unions were regulated, along with the individual labor contract, the financing structure, and the process of collective bargaining agreements. The establishment of the Labor Court and the Ministry of Labor completed the institutions of the system.

In terms of trade union structure, there is a monopoly of representation with regard to territorial coverage. The law determines that only a trade union may represent an economic category of workers (e.g., banking, metallurgical, and commerce workers) in the municipality where the companies are located. Only for federations and confederations, which bring together unions from the same state and from the entire country, is the creation of more than one entity permitted. The three main Brazilian trade union associations are *Central Única dos Trabalhadores* (CUT), *Força Sindical*, and *União Geral dos Trabalhadores* (UGT). Currently, CUT accounts for approximately 30 percent of Brazilian unions, and *Força Sindical* and UGT account for approximately 20 percent and 15 percent, respectively (Cardoso 2014). It is worth noting that, as in the case of Spain, trade union associations may have historical links to political parties. For example, the party alignment of the largest group of unionists of CUT is with the Workers' Party (PT).

Brazilian law does not guarantee the right of employee association at the workplace level. With this configuration, the industrial relations system in Brazil establishes trade union action always outside the organization. In some major companies works councils are recognized in collective bargaining, but their small number only reinforces the impression that, overall, the union is external to the organization.

Finally, union density in Brazil was only of 17 percent in 2013 (Rodrigues and Ramalho 2014). However, such low percentage is explained by the sources of funding of Brazilian trade unions, which we detail next.

Source of funding

Spain. In Spain, trade union results in works council elections, and hence "most representative" status, are also very important for financial reasons. Although unions obtain some income in the form of member dues (Köhler and Calleja Jiménez 2013), this is not their main source of funding. Instead, key resources come from public aid. Such financial aid is based on the number of delegates obtained in elections, as is the number of representatives trade unions may hold in different counseling bodies of state organs (Pérez-Yruela 1997). In addition, Spanish trade unions also obtain additional human resources depending on election results. By law, each elected delegate is granted a specific number of hours to deal with trade union-related work. More important, the law allows the bundling of the delegate hours of several delegates to release one person entirely from work at the company; that worker, instead, engages full-time in the service of the trade union (Köhler and Calleja Jiménez 2013).

Brazil. Brazilian labor legislation ensures trade unions an automatic annual transfer of funds known as union dues. This money is obtained as an annual tax on individuals, the value of which is equivalent to a workday of any formally employed Brazilian person, regardless of whether the employee is a union member or not. This mandatory fee makes trade unions largely independent from voluntary membership, even before the addition of monthly dues paid by union members.

Collective Bargaining

Spain. In Spain, since 2002, collective bargaining regulates a variety of issues, such as wage scales, working hours, training, and health and safety, and takes place at the national, industry and company levels. With the exception of 2009, an annual national agreement has provided a framework for lower-level bargaining at the firm level (Ministerio del Trabajo e Inmigración 2010). Until recently, the general pattern has been that large and medium-sized companies have their own agreements, sometimes at plant level, while smaller employers have been covered by provincial agreements for their industry (Fulton 2013). National-level agreements are usually "framework agreements" that do not regulate pay or working time, though they give broad guidelines. Company-level agreements, in turn, can regulate pay and working time by either setting out details in the agreement or by referring to a higher-level agreement (national or provincial) (Sanz de Miguel 2012). Percentage of employees covered by collective agreements in Spain is high (around 80%), which is due to the rule that agreements are generally binding (*erga omnes*), meaning that each company within the same industry or region is subject to its respective collective agreement. These agreements are legally binding for all firms; should a company violate collective agreement content, all individual contracts in such a company become invalid (Martín et al. 2006).

Despite the top-down nature of collective agreements, recent developments in Spanish legislation, motivated by the economic crisis of 2008 and the need for increasing flexibility in the labor market, have led both Socialist and Liberal Spanish governments to challenge the *erga omnes* nature of collective agreements. The most recent legislation in that respect is the Labor Market Reform law of 10 February 2012 (RD-Ley 3/2012), which establishes, among many other deregulation measures, that an employer can deviate from the collective agreement and introduce wage cuts or extend working time without negotiating with the works council, as long as the employer can provide "economic, technical, or competitive reasons" for doing so (Fulton 2013; Köhler and Calleja Jiménez 2013). In addition, firm-level collective agreements now take priority over industrywide collective agreements.

Brazil. In Brazil, there is no major nationwide agreement between workers and companies that established basic standards for bargaining at the regional, industry, or company level. Until the late 1980s, a centralized collective bargaining structure prevailed within the Brazilian industrial relations system (Pastore and Zylberstajn 1988), to the detriment of direct negotiations at the firm level. The negotiation is usually centralized, being held between the labor union or federation of a given segment of the economy and the industry trade union of that same segment. Although not as frequent, there are some collective bargaining agreements that result in nationwide agreements, as was the case in the banking sector. While the trade unions have pressured companies in sectors, such as the automotive, steel, and petrochemical industries, to negotiate national agreements, they have been met with fierce resistance (Amorim 2015).

In the mid-1990s, new legal regulations enabled firm-level negotiations in some specific areas, such as profit-sharing agreements and overtime rules (DIEESE, 2005). Such negotiations have become increasingly common, but almost always occur through the direct relationship between the union and the company, and rarely include the mediation or participation by an autonomous committee comprised of company workers (DIEESE 2012).

Union activity and influence

Spain. In addition to their presence in works councils, Spanish trade unions continue to have a strong capacity to mobilize both member and nonmember employees in strikes and similar protest actions. Although workplace conflict and strike activity has overall decreased since the late 1970s until today (Luque Balbona 2013), Spain continues to have one of the highest rates of strike frequency in Europe, with an annual average of approximately 140 days of work lost per 1,000 employees in the 2000–2010 period (Köhler and Calleja Jiménez 2013). Despite the number of strikes decreased in 2010 and 2011, in 2012 conflict rose again. There were 101 more industrial action incidents, and 101,897 more workers involved, in 2012 than in 2011 (Sanz de Miguel 2014). There was also an increase in strike activity in 2013 in comparison to 2012 (Ministerio de Empleo y Seguridad Social 2013). Interestingly, most of these strikes (62%) were at the company level and were called by workers' delegates and works councils.

Another proxy for trade unions' influence in Spain has to do with their participation in a variety of national-level economic debates and negotiations. Trade unions are partners in institutions such as "labor offices, social security, occupational training, universities, and economic and social councils" (Köhler and Calleja Jiménez 2013, 9). Social dialog with both the State and employer associations has been established over the years in such important matters as "economic and employment policy, pension reform, the health system and social dialogue in the public sector." Trade unions also play a social assistance role by implementing a variety of programs linked to immigration, equal opportunity, youth and gender integration, eradication of drug addiction, and the like (Cardeñosa 2010). This significant institutional role is explained in the case of Spain by the political role that trade unions played in the post-dictatorship era, as crucial stakeholders in the consolidation of the new democratic system (Pérez-Yruela 1997).

Brazil. Propositional strikes (i.e., those seeking better wages and working conditions for employees) increased in the period from 2003 to 2014 (Amorim 2015). The number of idle hours due to workers' strikes in Brazil rose from 15,805 in 2003 to 86,858 in 2012 (DIEESE 2013). These strikes involved both union members and nonmembers alike. Trade union influence was also felt in periods of greater severity in the labor market, such as the 1990s, when trade union associations were able to play a role as interlocutors with the federal government and entrepreneurs in national forums related to economic affairs or of interest to workers. At this stage, in addition to being propositional, the Brazilian trade union associations exercised veto power over public policy alternatives that displeased workers (Almeida 1998). Thus, whether in times of crisis or economic growth, it can be said that social dialog in Brazil involves trade union participation. In the 2000s, with economic growth and the advent of the government of Lula da Silva, the position of trade unions strengthened within the broader scenario of the country through the exercise of certain influence on the federal government itself. This was due to the presence of several former union leaders (especially from CUT) at various government levels, as well as in the National Congress itself (Baltar et al. 2010).

Spain and Brazil: A synthesis

As we have seen so far, Spanish and Brazilian industrial relations systems share some similarities. First, trade unions are maintained by dual funding sources: public funds and monthly fees of union workers, although public funds remain the more significant of the two sources. As a result, trade unions are less dependent on affiliation rates for their survival, which is shown in the low union density figures for both countries. Even with low union density, Spanish and Brazilian trade unions are relevant stakeholders in work related debates and negotiations both nationally and locally, mainly due to the activity of their main trade union associations. In Spain, they are involved with issues such as vocational training and the negotiation of changes in existing labor legislation. In Brazil, trade union associations participate in negotiations on the national minimum wage, sectoral stimulus policies, and debates on alternative forms of labor hiring in times of crisis. In both countries, trade unions are also crucial actors in collective bargaining. Finally, it should be noted that trade unions have organized a significant number of strikes in recent years both in Spain and Brazil.

Despite such similarities, significant differences in the Spanish and Brazilian industrial relations systems are also apparent. First, the organizational structures differ: in Spain, union bodies are present both inside and outside the firms, whereas in Brazil the organization of workers at the firm or workplace level is quite rare. The second major difference lies in how unions obtain public funding. In Spain, funding is linked to a union representativeness criterion (elected delegates at works councils), while in Brazil representativeness does not affect

TABLE 2
Spain and Brazil Industrial Relations Systems: Similarities and Differences

Similarities	*Differences*
– Public funding	– Union organizational structure
– Low union density	– Link between funding and representativeness
– Relevant stakeholders nationally and locally	– Scope of collective bargaining agreements
– Increased volume of strikes in recent years	

funding. By linking funding to representativeness, this criterion introduces what basically amounts to an incentive to union activity. The same cannot be said for Brazil, where the mandatory fee is collected regardless of membership, representativeness, or any other criteria related to union presence. Third, the national collective bargaining agreements are articulated by sector and by company in Spain, whereas in Brazil there is no articulation of these agreements at the industry or firm level; in addition, there are agreements covering the entire country, though these are rare. In Spain, specific agreements for large- or medium-sized companies are still possible, unlike in Brazil, where, as a general rule, agreements cannot be adapted to company size (Table 2).

METHODS

In the next section, using the 2014 Cranet survey, we compare data on the presence and influence exerted by trade unions in Spanish and Brazilian organizations as reported by HR specialists. We discuss these findings in the light of both countries' industrial relations systems.

Trade union influence in Spanish and Brazilian firms according to the 2014 Cranet survey

Sample

The data reported in this section come from Cranet, an international research network dedicated to analyzing HRM developments in public- and private-sector organizations with more than 100 employees within and across national contexts (Brewster, Mayrhofer, and Morley 2004). Data are collected by academics in different universities approximately every four years in more than 30 countries. Surveys that ask questions about HRM policies in different domains are filled out by HR specialists, more commonly HR managers in these organizations. The total number of organizations in the Spanish sample was 99, with a median number of 604 employees. Only 10.1 percent of the organizations in the Spanish sample belonged to the public sector. In Brazil, the sample is composed of 354 organizations with a median number of 850 employees. Only 12 percent of the Brazilian organizations belonged to the public sector.

TABLE 3

Trade Union Membership Rates in Surveyed Organizations (Percentage of
Organizations in Each Category)

Membership rate ranges	Spain	Brazil
0%	12	6
1%–10%	38	35
11%–25%	13	14
26%–50%	4	18
51%–75 %	7	7
76%–100%	1	17
Don't know	25	3
Total	100	100

Design

The data from the 2014 survey conducted in Spain and Brazil on the participation and influence of trade unions in the HR management of organizations have been divided into three blocks. The first one reports HR specialists' overall perception of the presence and influence of unions within their organizations. The second block reports data on trade union influence in salary negotiations and collective bargaining. Finally, we present data on the role played by trade unions in internal communication within these firms (both top down and bottom up).

Union Influence and Membership Rates

The survey asked the respondents to estimate union membership rate of their company's employees, as well as the level of influence exerted by unions within the organization. The results are shown on the tables below.

Table 3 shows that in both countries reported membership rates are low. In Spain, 50 percent of organizations report unionization rates below 10 percent, and in Brazil the figure is 41 percent. It is worth noting, however, that despite this similarity, percentages differ for the other membership rates for both countries. The first point to consider is that a quarter of the respondents from Spain claimed not to know the percentage of unionized employees in their company, whereas in Brazil only 3 percent did not give an estimate. Another relevant fact concerns the differences in the higher membership rates. Brazilian managers tended to give a higher estimate than their Spanish counterparts, including a significant difference in companies with nearly universal union membership—i.e., 76 percent to 100 percent of unionized workers—which was the case in 17 percent of Brazilian companies and only 1 percent of Spanish companies. It is unclear whether respondents confused mandatory union fees with unionization, or whether they really believe that membership is higher in Brazilian companies, but higher-rate numbers were also higher in Brazil.

In Table 4, it can be seen that the surveyed organizations in both countries consider unions to have a low degree of influence on them. In Spain and Brazil, 43 percent and 44 percent of organizations, respectively, reported that unions exert little or no influence on the

TABLE 4.
Trade union Influence Within the Organization According to HR Specialists
(Percentage of Surveyed Firms in Each Category)

Degree of influence	Spain	Brazil
No influence at all	20	4
1	23	40
2	30	29
3	20	17
Very large influence	7	10
Total	100	100

TABLE 5.
HR Managers Recognize the Importance of Trade Unions for the Purpose of
Collective Bargaining (In Percentage)

	Spain	Brazil
Recognizes	83	92
Does not recognize	17	8
Total	100	100

company's management. There are some differences between the two countries in the ranges between none and a great influence, but in this case they do not seem very significant.

Participation of Trade Unions in Salary Negotiation

Despite the low levels of union membership and reported influence, unions are nonetheless highly recognized as legitimate stakeholders in collective bargaining, as shown in Table 5 below. Hence, through collective bargaining, trade unions are able to influence working conditions (e.g., salary and working hours) within these firms.

Taken together, results from Tables 4 and 5 seem to indicate that while HR managers do not perceive a direct influence of unions on their daily work environment, many respondents recognize that trade unions play an important role in collective bargaining. This result suggests that, by virtue of law, unions are only seen as valid representatives when it is time to negotiate, rather than on a daily basis.

In order to analyze the participation and influence of the unions in the organizations, HR specialists were asked whether base pay negotiations took place collectively or individually—that is, whether negotiations involved the union or were held directly with each employee. In case of collective bargaining, they were also asked the level of these negotiations—that is, whether they were conducted at the national or regional levels, or by different companies and divisions belonging to the same corporate group.

Table 6 shows how the base wages of managers, professionals, and other employees (clerical or manual) are determined. It offers alternatives ranging from individual negotiation to national collective bargaining agreements. The results show that in Spain, for administrative

TABLE 6
Level at Which Basic Pay is Determined (Percentage of Surveyed Firms in Each Category)

	Spain			Brazil		
	Managers	Professional	Clerical or Manual	Managers	Professional	Clerical or Manual
National/industry wide collective bargaining	−27	39	61	36	28	29
Regional collective bargaining	8	22	38	46	59	68
Company/Division, etc.	78	69	50	14	11	10
Individual	77	64	37	39	27	21

and manual employees, wages are predominantly determined at the national level and secondarily at the company level. For managers and professionals, the negotiations are more likely to occur at the firm level and, at fairly close proportions, at the individual level. In the case of Brazilian organizations, salaries are predominantly determined through regional collective bargaining agreements, for all categories.

These results seem to be consistent with the general characteristics of the work systems shown in Table 1. This is because in Spain, two actors are important: national negotiations to define the minimum amount payable in organizations, and works councils assisting the negotiations of basic payments at the company level. It is also worth noting that individual negotiations of basic pay, characteristic of more competitive HRM models, are more common in Spain for all categories of employees.

As for Brazilian organizations, again consistent with the institutional description shown in Table 1, there is a predominance of regional negotiations, in which the prevailing role is that of the union with companies that are in its territorial base. In this sense, reflecting the low presence of trade unions at the company level, there is also a low participation of organizations claiming to determine the payment of managers, professionals, administrative and manual employees at the firm level.

Participation of Trade Unions in Company/Employee Communication

Tables 7 and 8 summarize data regarding the use of different methods or channels of communication used by management and employees to share their views on major workplace issues, as well as the extent to which trade union representatives and works councils are involved in such processes.

Table 7 shows that, in both Spain and Brazil, high percentages of organizations engage in direct contact or even in electronic communication as a way to connect with their employees. In Spain, however, it is more common for companies to communicate with their employees by holding regular meetings with the workforce and informational sessions with teams. The works council, an organization authority provided for by national legislation, is partially or

TABLE 7

Methods Used to Communicate Major Issues to Employees (Percentage of Organizations in Each Category)

METHODS	SPAIN Used to a great and very great extent	BRAZIL Used to a great and very great extent
Directly	86	60
Through trade union representatives	25	7
Through works councils	29	6
Regular workforce meetings	55	19
Team briefings	54	35
Electronic communication	89	71
Through immediate superior	81	72

TABLE 8

Methods Used by Employees to Communicate their Views to Managers (Percentage of Organizations in Each Category)

Method	Spain					Brazil				
	0 Not at all	1	2	3	4 To a very great extent	0 Not at all	1	2	3	4 To a very great extent
Through works councils	23	18	17	31	11	78	12	6	2	2
Direct to senior managers	2	4	24	41	28	27	16	19	14	24
Through immediate superior	2	4	24	41	28	8	5	18	24	45
Through trade union representatives	27	19	20	28	7	76	14	7	2	1
Through regular workforce meetings	11	14	38	29	9	60	10	15	7	7
Through team briefings	11	11	41	30	7	46	12	20	10	12
Through suggestion schemes	34	19	17	15	6	49	14	15	9	13
Through employee attitude surveys	14	21	21	27	18	58	14	16	8	4
Through electronic communication	7	13	20	38	23	31	13	17	16	24

largely adopted by almost 30 percent of organizations as a means of communication with workers.

Among Brazilian organizations, in contrast, the use of collective means of communication is virtually nonexistent. In high percentage, organizations rarely or never communicate with their employees through union representatives, works councils, or meetings with the workforce. Instead, managers of Brazilian organizations seem to have a strong preference for direct, vertical, electronic communication with workers or for routing information through the supervisor.

As for the communication flow that originates in the workers toward the organization, Table 8 shows that there is a greater variety of means of contact among Spanish organizations than among Brazilian ones. The means most commonly used by Spanish workers to express their ideas about work are direct contact with senior managers, contact through their immediate superiors, and electronic communication. Works councils and employee attitude surveys are also present in slightly over 40 percent of the organizations surveyed in Spain.

The bottom-up communication profile in Brazil appears to be completely different: here works councils and trade unions are very rarely used as communication channels between employee and organization. Only 4 percent of organizations make extensive use of surveys to gather employee perceptions about the job and the company. The hierarchical line appears to be the preferred way to listen to workers in Brazilian labor relations. For 70 percent of the organizations, contact with the immediate supervisor is used to a large or moderate extent, while 24 percent often rely on direct relations with senior managers, and 24 percent opt for the ease of electronic communication. Furthermore, many types of bottom-up communication are rated "Not at all" by Brazilian organizations.

Overall, Cranet data show that managers in Spain and Brazil rate the level of influence that trade unions exert in their organizations as low. Furthermore, according to surveyed HR specialists, there is a clear preference among both management and employees for direct and individualized communication. At the same time, we observe significant differences between the two countries, as salary negotiations at the organizational level are more common in Spain than in Brazil, and there is a larger diversity of communication channels between managers and employees in Spanish firms.

CONCLUSION

Despite some Cranet survey results (c.f. Tables 3 and 4) suggesting that trade unions may exert little influence in Spanish and Brazilian organizations, we have provided evidence to the contrary. An important fact is that the right of unions to exist and to organize is ensured and specified in the legislation. In a way, that means that the union does not have to rely exclusively on the legitimacy of its leadership with workers, and can limit its activities to negotiation time. Perhaps these are some of the reasons why HR professionals do not perceive unions as important components of their daily routines, such as the communication process. Union influence in these countries is exerted through their presence as negotiating partners in collective bargaining agreements, as well as through their power to call for strikes. In both cases, the influence of trade unions extends not only to their members, but also to nonmembers. The fact that trade unions remain strong in these countries is explained by the historical evolution of their industrial relations systems. In both cases, trade unions faced constant restrictions on their freedom of association in the period when the industrial relations system was being developed. Unions would sometimes try to circumvent these restrictions by organizing informally through shop-floor committees or inside the companies, while at other times they chose more open confrontation, with strikes and other mobilizations aimed at removing such restrictions. In a more general context, trade unions in both countries supported and participated in the movements for democracy, finding in politics an institutional environment that provided greater freedom of action. The legitimacy obtained both at the company level and at the broader institutional level has thrust trade unions into a leading role in their respective countries. Similarly, also in both countries, trade unions have always had strong relationships with political parties, thus resulting in a greater politicization of union and labor activity. Finally, in both countries unions were complementary players of the national political game in negotiations or discussions nationwide.

Such common factors help us explain some of the similarities that are encountered when comparing the roles that trade unions play today in both countries. For example, unions are legitimate actors in collective bargaining, with significant influence in the setting of wage levels for employees, especially in the case of administrative and manual workers. In addition, we have shown that trade union associations are regularly called to discuss major national issues that affect national labor markets with the government and employers, being therefore participants in the social dialog in their respective countries. Finally, trade unions continue to be partially funded by the State in both countries, and they play a pivotal role in work-related disputes and strikes.

An additional interesting finding from this study relates to the differences, rather than the similarities, that we observe in the Cranet data between Brazil and Spain. These differences relate to the role played by works councils in Spain, which do not have an equivalent organ in Brazil. Our data show that salary negotiations at the organizational level are more common in Spain than in Brazil, a difference that can be attributed to the existence of works councils in Spanish firms. In addition, works councils and trade unions still play a significant role as a communication channel with employees in Spanish firms, while their role is virtually non-existent in Brazil. Hence, due to the role played by works councils, we can see that trade unions influence Spanish firms from within, whereas in Brazil such influence is exerted from outside. Our analysis of the origins of the industrial relations systems in both countries helps us explain these differences, and provide some evidence of how particular events can have path-dependent effects that subtly, but also significantly, shape the evolution of HRM in both countries. For example, in Spain, Franco's decision to allow *de facto* the creation of shop-floor committees (Pérez-Yruela 1997) was the seed that later on evolved into the works councils that exist today. Over time, these councils became a very important channel for union influence. This did not happen in Brazil, where neither the Vargas government nor subsequent governments ever allowed the emergence of similar employee representative groups within organizations.

In sum, and despite the lack of longitudinal data in our Cranet dataset to offer support for either the convergence or divergence theses, our study emphasizes the importance of contextual factors in explaining HRM in both countries (e.g., Muller-Camen, Croucher, Flynn, and Schroder 2011). Interestingly, the similarities we find between Spain and Brazil in the role played by trade unions seem to be the result not so much of globalization, but of similar historical patterns in the development of their local industrial relations systems. Hence, while studies on the historical context of individual countries are still rare in the field of organizational studies (Clark and Rowlinson 2004), their results are potentially important for explaining how far the convergence between national HRM systems extends. Nevertheless, the low influence attributed to unions by the managers of organizations and the great emphasis on individualized communication also point to the same anti-union trends that are common in Anglo-Saxon cultures. A longitudinal analysis is needed to determine whether there are any long-term trends that support the supposedly lower influence of trade unions in these countries.

REFERENCES

Almeida, M. H. T. 1998. "Sindicatos em Tempos de Reforma." *São Paulo em Perspectiva, São Paulo-Fundação SEADE* 12 (1), 3–9.

Amorim, W. A. C. 2015. *Negociações Coletivas No Brasil: 50 Anos de Aprendizado*. São Paulo, Brazil: Editora Atlas.

Amorim, W. A. C., and L. S. Santos. 2012. "Greves no Brasil: Uma Análise do Período Recente e Tendências." In *Carta Social*. CESIT Unicamp.

Anner, M., and J. P. Cândia Veiga. 2013. "Brazil" In *Comparative Employment Relations in the Global Economy*, edited by C. Frege and J. Kelly, 265–85. London, UK and New York, NY: Routeledge.

Baltar, P. E. A., A. L. Santos, J. D. Krein, E. Leoni, M. W. Proni, A. Moreto, A. G. Maia, and C. Salas. 2010. "Moving towards Decent Work. Labor in the Lula Government: Reflections on Brazilian Experience." Global Labor University Working Paper, No. 9, International Labour Organization (ILO), Geneva.

Barbosa, A. F. 2008. *A formação do mercado de trabalho no Brasil*. São Paulo: Alameda.

Belizón, M., P. Gunnigle, M. Morley, and J. Lavelle. 2014. "Subsidiary Autonomy over Industrial Relations in Ireland and Spain." *European Journal of Industrial Relations* 20 (3):237–54. doi: 10.1177/0959680113517199.

Brewster, C. 2007. "Comparative HRM: European Views and Perspectives." *The International Journal of Human Resource Management* 18 (5):769–87. doi: 10.1080/09585190701248182.

Brewster, C., W. Mayrhofer and M. Morley (Eds.). 2004. *Human Resource Management in Europe: Evidence of Convergence?* Oxford, UK: Elsevier/Butterworth-Heinemann.

Cardeñosa, M. 2010. "Financiación y Recursos Humanos de Los Sindicatos." CCOO, Federación Servicios a la Ciudadanía. http://www.fsc.ccoo.es/comunes/recursos/99922/doc22211_Financiacion_y_recursos_humanos_de_CCOO.pdf

Cardoso, A. M. 2014. "Os Sindicatos No Brasil. Boletim Mercado de Trabalho: Conjuntura e Análise." *In Instituto de Pesquisa Econômica Aplicada* 20 (56):21–7.

Clark, P., and P. Rowlinson. 2004. "The Treatment of History in Organisation Studies: Towards an 'Historic Turn'?" *Business History* 46 (3):331–52. doi: 10.1080/0007679042000219175.

Comisiones Obreras (CCOO). 2013. *Memoria de Actividad - 10° Congreso Confederal*. Madrid: CCOO.

DIEESE. 2005. "Participação Dos Trabalhadores Nos Lucros ou Resultados Das Empresas." *Estudos e Pesquisas, São Paulo* 3 (22), 1–25.

DIEESE. 2012. *A Situação Do Trabalho No Brasil*. São Paulo, Brazil: DIEESE.

DIEESE. 2013. "Balanço das Greves em 2012." Estudos e Pesquisas n°66. Brazil: DIEESE, 1–35.

Economic Commission for Latin America and the Caribbean (ECLAC). 2016. Foreign Direct Investment in Latin America and the Caribbean. 2016 (LC/G.2680-P). Santiago, Chile: Economic Commission for Latin America and the Caribbean.

Elvira, M. M., and A. Davila. 2005. "Emergent Directions for Human Resource Management Research in Latin America." *The International Journal of Human Resource Management* 16 (12):2265–82. doi: 10.1080/09585190500358703.

European Parliament and of the Council. 2009. "Directive 2009/38/EC." Official Journal of the European Union (122/28) 16.5. Aberdeen: European Union.

Ferner, A., and J. Quintanilla. 2002. "Between Globalization and Capitalist Variety: Multinationals and the International Diffusion of Employment Relations." *European Journal of Industrial Relations* 8 (3):243–50. doi: 10.1177/095968010283002.

Fulton, L. 2013. "Worker Representation in Europe." Labor Research Department and ETUI http://www.worker-participation.eu/National-Industrial-Relations.

Hall, P. and Soskice, D. (eds.). 2003. *Varieties of Capitalism – The Institutional Foundations of Comparative Advantage*. Oxford: Oxford Press.

International Labor Office (ILO). 2014. "Case No. 2947 (Spain): Report in which the Committee Requests to be Kept Informed of Developments." *371st report of the committee on freedom of association*, 317–465.

Jevtić, M. 2012. The Role of Works Councils and Trade Unions in Representing Interests of the Employees in EU Member States (Partnership or Competition). Belgrade, Serbia: Friedrich Ebert Stiftung.

Jódar, P., R. Alòs, P. J. Beneyto, and O. Molina. 2012. "Una Breve Panorámica de Las Elecciones Sindicales 2011, Con Apuntes Sobre su Evolución Desde 2003." *In Anuario Sociolaboral de la Fundación 1° de Mayo* 8:541–57.

Köhler, H.-D., J. P. Calleja Jiménez. 2013. *Trade Unions in Spain. Organisation. Environment, Challenges,* 1–18. Berlin, Germany: Friedrich Ebert Stifung Studies.

Lucena, H., and A. Covarrubia. 2006. "Industrial Relations in Latin America." In *Global Industrial Relations,* edited by D. G. Collings, M.J. Morley and P. Gunnigle, 53–70. New York, NY: Routledge.

Luque Balbona, D. 2013. "La Forma de Las Huelgas en España 1905–2010." *Política y Sociedad* 50 (1):235–68. doi: 10.5209/rev_POSO.2013.v50.n1.37554.

Martín, A., B. Ríos, F. Ferrando, and M. A. Limón. 2006. "Collective Agreements." Paper presented at XIVth Meeting of European Labor Court Judges, Paris, France.

Mayrhofer, W., and C. Brewster. 2005. "European Human Resource Management: Researching Developments over Time." *Management Revu* 16 (1):36–62. doi: 10.5771/0935-9915-2005-1-36.

Mitchell, R., and J. Fetter. 2003. "Human Resource Management and Individualisation in Australian Law." *Journal of Industrial Relations* 45 (3):292–325. doi: 10.1111/1472-9296.00085.

Ministerio de Empleo y Seguridad Social. 2013. "Conflictos Desarrollados en 2013." http://www.empleo.gob.es/estadisticas/hue/hue13/HU1/index.htm

Ministerio del Trabajo e Inmigración. 2010. *Encuesta de Calidad de Vida en el Trabajo.* http://www.empleo.gob.es/estadisticas/ecvt/welcome.htm

Morley, M., C. Brewster, P. Gunnigle, and W. Mayrhofer. 1996. "Evaluating Change in European Industrial Relations: Research Evidence on Trends at Organisational Level." *The International Journal of Human Resource Management* 7 (3):640–56. doi: 10.1080/09585199600000148.

Muller-Camen, M., R. Croucher, M. Flynn, and H. Schroder. 2011. "National Institutions and Employers' Age Management Practices in Britain and Germany: 'Path Dependence' and Option Exploration." *Human Relations* 64 (4):507–30. doi: 10.1177/0018726710396246.

Nelson, R. 1996. *The Sources of Economic Growth.* Boston, MA: Harvard University Press.

Pastore, J., and H. Zylberstajn. 1988. *A Administração Do Conflito Trabalhista No Brasil.* São Paulo, Brazil: Instituto de Pesquisas Econômicas.

Pérez-Yruela, M. 1997. "Trade Unions and Industrial Relations in Spain (1975–1994): From Old to New Practices." CIBS Research Papers in International Business. London, UK: London South Bank University, 1–44.

Pla-Barber, J., and J. Camps. 2012. "Springboarding: A new geographical landscape for European foreign investment in Latin America." *Journal of Economic Geography,* Oxford University Press 12 (2):519–538.

Rodrigues, I. J., and R. Ramalho. 2014. "Novas Configurações Do Sindicalismo No Brasil? Uma Análise a Partir Do Perfil Dos Trabalhadores Sindicalizados." *Revista de Sociologia da UFSCAR* 4 (2):381–403.

Sanz de Miguel, P. 2012. "Spain: Industrial Relations Profile." In Observatory European Observatory of Working Life. Dublin, Ireland: European Foundation for the Improvement of Living and Working Conditions. http://www.eurofound.europa.eu/observatories/eurwork/comparative-information/national-contributions/spain/spain-industrial-relations-profile

Souza, C. P. S., K. D. D. Roglio, S. W. S. Renwick, and A. R. W. Takahashi. 2014. "Contemporary Trends in Brazilian Human Resource Management Studies over the Last Decade (2001–2010)." *International Business Research* 7 (8):29–46. doi: 10.5539/ibr.v7n8p29.

Storey, J., and N. Bacon. 1993. "Individualism and Collectivism: Into the 1990s." *International Journal of Human Resource Management* 4 (3):665–84. doi: 10.1080/09585199300000042.

Visser, J., S. Hayter, and R. Gammarano. 2015. "Trends in Collective Bargaining Coverage: Stability, Erosion or Decline?" *Labour Relations and Collective Bargaining Policy Brief No. 1.* Geneva, Switzerland: ILO.

The Antecedents of Comparative Differences in Union Presence and Engagement: Evidence from Coordinated and Liberal Market Contexts

Michael Brookes, Geoffrey Wood and Chris Brewster

Abstract: This study employs a large on-going survey database to explore the antecedents of comparative differences in union representation and the extent to which employers engage with them at the workplace, and how this has changed over time. It finds that amongst organizations employing more than 100 employees, there has been no uniform decline in the presence of unions, or engagement by employers with them at the workplace. In other words, although we do not measure the range of topics covered or the impact of such engagement, it is clear that neither the neo-liberal nor the more critical theory suggestions that systems are naturally converging to a common model of minimal union presence and engagement receives much support. Collective employment relations are influenced by comparative capitalisms and, to a lesser extent, legal systems and remain a significant feature of many continental European economies.

INTRODUCTION

There is a growing body of international literature that focuses on the effects of institutional mediation on employment relations practice, and on possible trends to convergence (Brewster et al. 2006; Lane and Wood 2009; Mayrhofer, Brewster, Morley and Ledolter 2011). Much of the literature outlining and contrasting employment relations practices only looks at a particular point of time. Clearly, to draw any conclusions about possible convergence, it is important either to have data from different times or to have data that looks back over time. Much of the extant literature confuses what are two different concepts when discussing convergence (see Mayrhofer and Brewster 2005; Mayrhofer et al. 2002). The dictionary defines convergence as existing when the analyzed variables develop over time in a way that would, eventually, lead to a common end point: the differences between the units—countries in our analysis—decrease. According to Friedman (1992, 2130), "the real test of a tendency to convergence would be in showing a consistent diminution of variance." Sometimes convergence is confused with the other concept: similar trends. This type of "convergence" occurs when the developments of variables in units of analysis over time are pointing in the same direction. Thus, pertinently for our analysis here, it is well known both that the membership of trade unions is declining in most countries over the last 25 years, but also that there is some consistency in differences between countries in their levels of union membership (Checchi and Visser 2005; Hall and Soskice 2001): there is evidence of common trends but no evidence of convergence. The distinction is important because it explains the danger of drawing conclusions from similar trends as if they are evidence of convergence.

We draw upon successive waves of an international survey of HR managers, in order to explore tendencies and changes, comparing and contrasting these with the predictions of the socioeconomic and employment relations literature. A key aim of this research is to explore the extent to which there has been a shift away from collectivism and to assess the antecedents of any such change in different institutional contexts. More specifically, we explore the extent to which there has been a move towards nonunionism across larger organizations in the developed world, epitomized by a decline in collective employment relations. We find the persistence of diversity but, at the same time, evidence of uneven and varied change in specific contexts. We locate this finding within recent developments in the socioeconomic literature.

Convergence and Diffusion as a Product of Union Decline

In an influential book, Katz and Darbishire (2000) explored the extent to which national employment relations practices are converging, based on a cross-section of developed Western European, Far Eastern, and North American economies. They found a persistence of difference but suggested that diversity was growing within all national economies and sectors; at the same time, they encountered a common trend to weaker unions, and centralized bargaining, and heterogeneity in pay systems (Katz and Darbishire 2000; Marsden et al. 2001, 683). They conclude that collective bargaining has become heterogeneous between and within countries (Katz and Darbishire 2000). In other words, not only has the basis of union representation—and the extent to which employers engage with them—eroded, but there is also greater diversity in the form the latter assumes. A range of other arguments support this point of view, and/or are even more explicitly pessimistic. For example, Turner (2009) notes that the use of new strategies by German unions points to the extent to which institutional stability cannot be assumed and that action by key players can impact on the broader system (c.f. Colvin 2003).

Moody (1997) argues that there has been a general convergence around the hardline anti-union practices. There is evidence that unions have become much weaker even in contexts where historically they were quite strong. For example, Doellgast, Holtgrewe, and Deery (2009) argue that, in conjunction with the works council system, unions remain effective in

Germany in supporting worker rights, but that outsourcing is a mechanism for firms to opt out from some of the imposed strictures. In turn, the latter might undermine the position of unions across society. Looking at the German context, Turner (2009) argues that an over-reliance on institutional supports has made for complacency in the trade unions. In short, union representation and the extent to which employers engage with them have both declined.

Other writers, such as Godard (2006), have argued that the trend towards a decline in union representation and collective bargaining reflects the actions of neo-liberal governments and the general hegemony of neo-liberal ideologies. Marsden et al. (2001) argues that there are some brakes on this process: renegotiation of the terms and conditions of work and employment and how they are negotiated undermine implicit rules and, on an individual basis, erode trust. In contrast, the retention of a collective element allows for meaningful compromises by both sides, even if the price is the erosion of some flexibility. Godard (2003) cautions against the view that convergence towards low labor standards are inevitable; it is possible, for example, for law to arrest or accelerate this process, citing the differences between the USA and Canada. This would suggest that national institutional systems are quite resilient. Indeed, there is recent evidence from Europe that the process of liberalization in coordinated markets may be over-estimated; for example, Thelen (2014) highlights the relative resilience of the German model and the underlying basis of collectivism. In other words, there has been a persistence of difference in both union representation and the extent to which employers engage with them. This raises the question as to whether national institutional factors exert a persistently different effect on national employment relations practice.

Persistent Differences: The Varieties of Capitalism Literature

The Varieties of Capitalism (VoC) literature (Hall and Soskice 2001) argues that there are persistent differences between Liberal Market Economies (LMEs) (i.e., the developed Anglo-Saxon economies) and Coordinated Market Economies (i.e., the Rhineland economies, Scandinavia, and Japan).

A central concept in the VoC literature is that of complementarity: in other words, that specific institutional forms and combinations of practices work together better than they would on their own. This allows systems to build on their respective strengths and, indeed, to compensate for any inherent weaknesses (Crouch 2005). Other strands of the VoC literature, which may currently have some resonance, have argued that liberal markets are excessively short-term, a fact that has ultimately detrimental consequences for firms and their stakeholders (c.f. Lincoln and Kalleberg 1990; Dore 2000). In LMEs, shareholder value has primacy: this means that firms will orientate their activities to short term returns. Whilst this may make for labor repression, it may also facilitate high-technology activities with generically skilled highly mobile workforces (Thelen 2001). Central to liberal market economies is insecure and individualized employment contracting (Hall and Soskice 2001; Tregaskis and Brewster 2006). In CMEs, different stakeholder interests are reconciled to a very greater extent: they work on compromise, rather than as a zero-sum game, underpinned by a greater emphasis on centralized bargaining and tradeoffs. This, in turn, makes for more cooperative work and employment relations, characterized by security of tenure, organization-specific human capital development, and collective voice mechanisms (Brewster et al. 2007).

The CME/LME categories are quite broad; other accounts have drawn attention to many more varieties of capitalism (Amable 2003; Whitley 1999). Amable (2003, 104–5) focuses particularly on the case of continental Europe, drawing a distinction between "continental European" (NW European "Rhineland" capitalism), and social democratic (or Scandinavian[1]) capitalism. The latter category differs partly in that a weaker security of tenure is often compensated for by a greater emphasis on often-state-sponsored continuous skills development, and, above all, through persistently higher levels of collective representation.

More recent developments and extensions of the VoC literature point to the uneven, episodic and often experimental nature of systemic change (Hollingsworth 2006; Lane and Wood 2009). It is evident that both coordinated varieties of capitalism and neo-liberal economies have had to face the possibility of far reaching changes in regulation and practice. Recent work has highlighted the effects of politics (Hancke, Rhodes, and Thatcher 2007), and the process of experimentation. In practice, change may be about hybridization (the mixing of practices from different models (as is taking place in CMEs), or "endo-metabalizm," internal development, for example, in LMEs becoming ever more extreme (Boyer 2006, 54). As Teague argues, this means that radical systemic change is unlikely; change is more likely to be incremental, uneven and open ended. In short, what the most recent literature on comparative capitalism suggests is that even as national archetypes have evolved, and although there is a general trend towards liberalization, the relative differences between them have persisted: if CMEs have liberalized, LMEs have become ever more extreme versions of themselves.

The overall theme underpinning all of this is that the union presence, and the degree of their formal engagement with employers, represents a function of the environment in which they operate, and how it is changing. A key issue still remains unresolved: how the behavior of unions and firms might be expected to evolve within differing environments. Clearly, within a framework more conducive to unions, they are more likely to secure a place at the workplace, and employers are likely to be more willing to communicate and exchange views through the trade union representatives. As a consequence, these factors will form the basis of our empirical measure of union presence, and their degree to which employers will formally engage with them.

Statement of Hypotheses

Drawing on the above discussion of theories of comparative difference and change, we offer a number of hypotheses. First, it can be argued that there is a general tendency towards union decline, with this being evidenced by both a fall in union membership as well as employers being less willing to engage with them. This is reflected in the reduced efficacy of the institutional supports of representation (Turner 2009).

Hypothesis 1: There is a trend towards a general decline in both union presence, and in the relative willingness of employers to engage with them, regardless of national institutional setting.

Alternatively, it can be argued that any changes are likely to be modest and unlikely to constitute ruptures from established ways of doing things. Different types of capitalism are likely to retain their distinct characteristics (Thelen 2009): the unionization and employer engagement with unions remains persistently higher in CMEs.

Hypothesis 2a: There are ongoing differences in both union presence and the relative willingness of employers to engage with them across institutional settings such that CME firms show higher levels of union presence and greater willingness of employers to engage with them relative to their LME counterparts.

In moving beyond the LME and CME archetypal models, Amable (2003) argues that employment relations practices are likely to differ not only between liberal market economies and more coordinated ones but, within the latter category, between (Scandinavia) social democratic capitalism and continental European capitalism. In the latter, unions will not be quite as strong as in the (Scandinavian) social democracies, given differences in both their legal environments and social conventions (Amable 2003). Hence, we have the following hypothesis:

Hypothesis 2b: There are ongoing differences in union presence, and in the relative willingness of employers to engage with them between LMEs, continental European and social democratic capitalism, with unions weakest in LMEs and strongest in social democracies.

An alternative view is that rather than a status quo, there has been a general decline in the presence of unions within the workplace, albeit that the level of unionization has persisted in proportionate terms. In other words, whilst systems are retaining differences, all are liberalizing, making for a general picture of union decline. Hence, we have the following hypothesis:

Hypothesis 3: Although there is a general trend towards decline in both union presence and in the relative willingness of employers to engage with them, the relative difference between various types of capitalism has persisted.

METHODOLOGY

We assess variations in the relationship between institutions and employment relations through using the repeating Cranet survey of senior HR managers, which now contains evidence on policies and practices within private and public sector organizations in most European countries (Brewster, Mayrhofer, and Morley 2004). The use of management-sourced information to focus on a single issue, changes in union-organization relations, is not unproblematic. In particular, it limits our ability to report explicit practice within the organization and to assess employee perceptions. However, in return, it enables us to compare organizational level policies across a range of different countries and, hence, institutional settings. Cranet only covers organizations with more than 100 employees; the exclusion of smaller organizations means that trends in that area are not covered, making for rather different results to national level surveys such as the *Workplace Employment Relations Survey* in the UK. However, given that unions are more likely to be represented in larger firms, Cranet does provide particularly valuable insights into the effects of union decline in this area.

Sampling

The data set used here cover five waves of the Cranet survey (i.e., 1991; 1995; 1999/2000; 2003/4; and 2009). The data for each country are representative with respect to size of industrial sectors by employment, with each subsequent cross-sectional wave being adjusted to reflect changes in the relative size of industrial sectors (Brewster et al. 2007). Thus, the sample remains representative across the whole period considered. For the purpose of this study, data from the UK, Germany, and Sweden are used to test our hypotheses: in each case representing the largest European example of a liberal market economy, continental European capitalism, and social democratic capitalism, respectively. Beyond this, the UK is regularly held up as the quintessential LME in Europe, and Germany is seen as the archetypical continental European CME. Indeed, in some of the key varieties of capitalism texts (for example, Hall and Soskice 2001; Thelen 2009) the discussion is almost as much about Germany as it is about coordinated market economies. The German economy makes up a hugely disproportionate percentage of the general discussion about CMEs. Among the Scandinavian social democracies, flexicurity (Wilthagen and Tros 2004) is less advanced in Sweden, which arguably, makes it similarly the most quintessential example of a Scandinavian social democracy. Denmark is typically held up as a flexicurity economy and, hence, is atypical of the category. Sweden is not only a larger economy but more typical than Denmark.

The data include 9,359 observations, with the breakdown by country and year as reported below in Table 1. Although the data are skewed towards the UK, with over half of the sample from UK firms, the sub-samples for each country in each year remain representative by industrial sector.

TABLE 1
Breakdown of Data Sample

Year	UK	Germany	Sweden	Total
1991	1,508	967	295	2770
1995	1,178	383	344	1,905
1999	1,091	503	352	1,946
2003	1,115	320	383	1,818
2009	218	420	282	920
Total	5,110	2,593	1,656	9,359

Model

The empirical analysis explores the relationship between (1) union representation and (2) the relative willingness of employers to engage with them, as well as time and different national settings. For the purpose of the empirical model, a scale is created that simultaneously captures both of these and reflects the extent of union power and influence within the organization. For this purpose, a Mokken non-parametric scale is constructed from the binary responses to 4 key questions, as follows: (1) Are over 50% of employees members of a union? (2) Does management perceive that unions have an influence within the organization? (3) Does management communicate to employees on key issues through trade union representatives? and (4) Do employees communicate their views to management through trade union representatives?

Fifty percent is, in many national contexts, the legal benchmark for trade union representivity and recognition (Wilkinson, Wood, and Deeg 2014). In addition to collective bargaining, engagement with unions may involve ongoing communications; alternatively, the use of nonunion forms of communication may dilute the role of unions (Brewster et al. 2007). The scale is weighted to reflect the proportion of positive responses to each question, and the resultant scale is a continuous variable ranging from 0 to 100, with higher values indicating that unions have greater scope to influence activities and decisions within that firm. The union influence scale is then used as the dependent variable within an Ordinary Least Squares (OLS) regression model.

Union representation and employer engagement with them within the firm is estimated as a function of both time and country, enabling the three hypotheses to be tested. Dummy variables are created for each country, with the UK as the reference category and, for the four survey years, using 1991 as the base group. In addition, situational variables are included to reflect a range of factors likely to influence the extent of union representation and the extent to which employers engage with them at the workplace. These are: Firm's size, measured by the number of employees, since it is anticipated that larger firms are broadly more likely to engage with representative bodies; Sector, with a dummy variable indicating those organizations in the public sector, the expectation being that a union presence is more prevalent within the public sector, hence there is likely to be a positive correlation between the public sector dummy and union representation and the extent to which employers engage with them at the workplace; and finally, Industry, since it is likely that trade union representation, and the extent to which employers engage with them at the workplace, lends itself to typical modes of production in different industries.

So a set of 15 industry dummies are included with metal manufacturing being used as the base group. The overall reference category chosen for the model is a private sector metal manufacturing company in the UK in 1991. The rationale here is that the UK represents the archetypical LME (i.e., an advanced case of one of the two mature varieties of capitalism), and 1991 represents the first year of data gathering for this study. Moreover, metal manufacturing was traditionally core to the manufacturing sector and remains heavily unionized (Doyle 1985).

FINDINGS

The purpose of the empirical model is to estimate representativity/engagement (RE) using a single measure, and Table 2 records the key elements of the Mokken scale, constructed from each firms' responses to the four questions relating to RE. With a Cronbach's alpha greater than 0.7 and all of the Loevinger's H-coefficients greater than 0.3 as well as each of the correlations being greater than 0.3, it is clear that the data is within the acceptable range for both reliability and scalability. As a result, it is a statistically valid step to use these measures to construct the Mokken scale, with the resultant scale being used as the dependent variable in the empirical model.

Table 3 records the mean values of the RE scale by year and country. The first hypothesis posits that there has been a decline in RE over the period of 1991–2019 and that national systems have become more alike. However, although we found a general decline in representation and the extent of employer engagement with them, important national differences have persisted; Hypothesis 1 is therefore not supported. Hypothesis 2a proposed that the different types of economy were likely to be distinct in terms of the extent of RE; we found that this was indeed the case. However, a closer evaluation revealed much diversity within the CME category: the decline in RE was more pronounced in Germany (continental European CME) and the UK (LME) than in Sweden (social democratic capitalism), thus confirming Hypothesis 2b. Not only were there persistent differences between LMEs and CMEs, but there were also considerable differences within the CME category.

The UK and Germany are within a similar range in terms of the relative decline of RE in evidence. However, in the case of Swedish firms, while a decline is in evidence, it is slower

TABLE 2

Mokken Scale of union representation and the extent to which employers engage with them at the workplace (RE)

		Mean	H_{wgt}	Corr.
Scale	Overall calculative scale, 4 items (Cronbach's alpha = 0.72)		0.71	0.41
Item 1	>50% union membership	0.38	0.83	0.39
Item 2	Perceive union has influence	0.82	0.69	0.57
Item 3	Management communicate through TU reps	0.81	0.60	0.48
Item 4	Employees communicate views through TU reps	0.72	0.74	0.65

TABLE 3
Mean Values of RE Scale

Year	UK	Germany	Sweden	Total
1991	60.98	58.86	94.21	63.78
1995	58.57	58.82	95.09	65.21
1999	45.82	49.77	92.91	55.36
2003	39.33	40.73	90.01	50.25
2009	26.15	31.23	84.64	46.40
Total	50.98	50.38	91.52	58.76

than the decline in the UK and Germany. We cannot, therefore, conclude that the decline is occurring at broadly the same rate; so, Hypothesis 3 is not supported.

Before these findings can be confirmed, the extent to which RE reflects the situation faced by each individual firm needs to be established. Table 4 presents the results from estimating a regression model of RE as a function of a series of situational variables, plus time and country. The level of RE is significantly greater in public sector organizations, though this is not evident with respect to firm size. There is no evidence that larger firms experience greater RE. RE also varies across industries with some being more, or less, favorable to union activities. Within the model, a number of industries have significantly lower levels of RE than the metal manufacturing reference category (see Table 4).

Finally, the findings remain largely unaffected once the impact of the situational variables has been controlled for. There is a significant reduction in the level of RE between 1991 and 2009, and the size of that reduction increases wave by wave, but this has not led to broad similarity across national boundaries, as was suggested by H1. Sweden is significantly

TABLE 4
OLS model of RE

Variable	Coefficient	t-Ratio	Mean
Constant	63.34***	74.58	
Total employees (000's)	0.00	1.03	3.98
Public sector	14.69***	13.63	0.21
Agriculture, hunting, forestry, fishing	−14.30***	−4.18	0.01
Energy and water	1.49	0.84	0.03
Chemical products	−3.51**	−2.25	0.04
Other manufacturing	1.54	1.56	0.16
Building and civil engineering	−17.26***	−9.92	0.03
Retail and distribution	−22.56***	−18.34	0.08
Transport and communication	−4.26***	−2.78	0.05
Banking, finance, insurance	−27.39***	−24.52	0.11
Personal, domestic, recreational services	−30.92***	−8.18	0.01
Health services	−1.68	−1.00	0.05
Other services	−13.63***	−9.16	0.05
Education	−5.72***	−3.25	0.04
Public Administration	−3.98***	−2.66	0.09
Other	−9.97***	−6.56	0.05
1995	−1.71**	−2.05	0.21
1999	−10.25***	−12.10	0.20
2003	−16.22***	−18.47	0.19
2009	−22.70***	−19.88	0.09
Germany	0.721	0.99	0.28
Sweden	39.92***	48.00	0.18
Dependent Variable	RE Scale		
Mean	58.76		
Observations	9359		
R-squared	0.37		
F Stat.	237.06		

*, **, and *** denote significance at the 10%, 5%, and 1% levels, respectively.

different from the UK with the German dummy being a long way from achieving any meaningful level of significance; in other words, whilst there was persistent difference between LMEs and CMEs, as suggested by H2a, a closer analysis revealed that much of the difference was due to the Swedish case, highlighting the nature of diversity with the CME category, as suggested by H2b. In short, we found that national systems were all changing, in the same direction but not at a similar rate: there was difference, but the gap between different national systems varied with time since, as discussed earlier the patterns of change are very different in Sweden than in the UK and Germany, and, thus, suggesting that we cannot accept H3.

DISCUSSION AND CONCLUSION

This study of a large number of organizations with more than 100 employees across three crucial economies found that, at least amongst these larger organizations, there is little evidence of a convergence in practices. As such, it disproves both neo-liberal (e.g. Hansmann and Kraakman 2003) and more critical (e.g. Katz and Darbishire 2000) theories that systems are naturally converging on to a common model of weak unions and little in the way of collective bargaining. Rather, we found that context continues to mold both the incidence of unions and collective bargaining and mitigate (or accelerate) their decline. In this respect, a core institutional feature of social democratic capitalism is considerably more resilient than often predicted. Conversely, the decline of collective representation in an example of an LME has been particularly pronounced; employment relations in different national systems are not all individualizing at the same rate. The differences between Scandinavia and the continental European Rhineland economies would also highlight the limitations of dichotomous VoC models.

We conclude that Amable's (2003) multi-variety model of capitalism was a more accurate predictor of the incidence and nature of collective representation than a simple dichotomous one; there are, as he suggests, some important differences between what goes on in the Scandinavian social democracies and in continental/"Rhineland" Europe. In addition, different national systems are changing at different rates. Although we found evidence of individualization in Germany, as suggested in other accounts (Streeck 2001), some of our findings support other studies indicating that in other areas, such as the market for corporate control and training, the national model has been strengthened, not weakened (Thelen 2014).

The comparative capitalisms literature is developing, but the basic principle that models are distinct and unlikely to lose their distinction seems to have some validity. This would suggest that national institutions are not closely or perfectly coupled, and that reform is possible in one area without endangering systemic coordination in another. This highlights the complex nature of capitalist diversity (Walker, Brewster, and Wood 2014), and the fundamental distinctions that persist between mature institutional environments. Clearly the decline of collectivism has been significantly affected by the socioeconomic conditions of the specific countries and there seems to be little evidence of convergence. Despite being the product of a clear failure of neo-liberalism, the 2008-economic crisis appears to have accelerated the pace of neo-liberal reforms across a wide range of national contexts; yet, there remains little sign of coherent convergence. This study only looks at a single defining feature of national contexts; however, changes in other areas suggest contradictory and uneven pressures in any tendencies to systemic liberalization. Not only are national systems evolving in complex and dynamic fashions, but the relative pace of change varies between national settings.

It may be that smaller organizations not included in our database do not follow the pattern of the larger exemplars: Perhaps the most significant limitation on our data is that we are restricted to organizations with more than 100 employees. This, however, in one sense strengthens our argument. As Roberts (2003, 37) notes, in most small firms, union penetration is minimal, and the process of interaction between managers and workers is informal. Further, our data are drawn from the most senior executive in each organization: arguably, they might be the people who would have the best access to the necessary data and the deepest knowledge of organizational HRM policies (Huselid and Becker 2000), but it would be valuable in future research to check their perceptions against those of trade union leaders and members. However, despite these limitations, the findings do allow us to draw significant conclusions about the comparative capitalisms antecedents of developments in unionization.

Note

1. In fact, he uses all the Nordic countries in his Scandinavian category.

REFERENCES

Amable, B. 2003. *The Diversity of Modern Capitalism*. Oxford, UK: Oxford University Press.
Boyer, R. 2006. "How do Institutions Cohere and Change." In *Institutions, Production and Working Life*, edited by G. Wood and P. James, 13–61. Oxford, UK: Oxford University Press.
Brewster, C., G. Wood, R. Croucher, and M. Brookes. 2007. "Collective and Individual Voice: Convergence in Europe?" *The International Journal of Human Resource Management* 18 (7):1246–62. doi:10.1080/09585190701393582.
Brewster, C., M. Brookes, and G. Wood. 2006. "Varieties of Firm." In *Institutions, Production and Working Life*, edited by G. Wood and P. James, 217–34. Oxford, UK: Oxford University Press.
Brewster, C., W. Mayrhofer, and M. J. Morley. (eds.). 2004. *Human Resource Management in Europe: Evidence of Convergence?* London, UK: Butterworth Heinemann.
Checchi, D., and J. Visser. 2005. "Pattern Persistence in European Trade Union Density: A Longitudinal Analysis 1950–1996." *European Sociological Review* 21 (1):1–21. doi:10.1093/esr/jci001.
Colvin, A. J. S. 2003. "Institutional Pressures, Human Resource Strategies, and the Rise of Nonunion Dispute Resolution Procedures." *ILR Review* 56 (3):375–92. doi:10.1177/001979390305600301.
Crouch, C. 2005. "Three Meanings of Complementarity." *Socio-Economic Review* 3 (2):359–63. doi:10.1093/SER/mwi015.
Doellgast, V., U. Holtgrewe, and S. Deery. 2009. "The Effects of National Institutions and Collective Bargaining Arrangements on Job Quality in Front-Line Service Workplaces." *ILR Review* 62 (4):489–509. doi:10.1177/001979390906200402.
Dore, R. 2000. *Stock Market Capitalism: Welfare Capitalism*. Cambridge, UK: Cambridge University Press.

Doyle, P. M. 1985. "Area Wage Surveys Shed Light on Declines in Unionization." *Monthly Labor Review* 108: 13–20.

Friedman, M. 1992. "Do Old Fallacies Ever Die?" *Journal of Economic Literature* 30 (4):2129–32.

Godard, J. 2003. "Do Labor Laws Matter? the Density Decline and Convergence Thesis Revisited." *Industrial Relations* 42 (3):458–92. doi:10.1111/1468-232X.00300.

Godard, J. 2006. "The US and Canadian Unions: Markets vs States and Society." In *Trade Unions and Democracy*, edited by M. Harcourt and G. Wood, 159–90. Manchester, UK: Manchester University Press.

Hall, P., and D. Soskice. 2001. "An Introduction to the Varieties of Capitalism." In *Varieties of Capitalism: The Institutional Basis of Competitive Advantage*, edited by P. Hall and D. Soskice, 21–7. Oxford, UK: Oxford University Press.

Hancke, B., M. Rhodes, and M. Thatcher. 2007. "Introduction: Beyond Varieties of Capitalism." In *Beyond Varieties of Capitalism*, edited by B. Hancke, M. Rhodes, and M. Thatcher, 1–41. Oxford, UK: Oxford University Press.

Hansmann, H., and R. Kraakman. 2003. "The End of History for Corporate Law." In *Convergence and Persistence in Corporate Governance*, edited by J. Gordon and M. Roe, 49–78. Cambridge, UK: Cambridge University Press.

Hollingsworth, J. R. 2006. "Advancing our Understanding of Capitalism with Niels Bohr's Thinking about Complementarity." In *Institutions and Working Life*, edited by P. James and G. Wood, 62–82. Oxford, UK: Oxford University Press.

Huselid, M. A., and B. E. Becker. 2000. "Comment on 'Measurement Error in Research on Human Resources and Firm Performance: How Much Error Is There and How Does It Influence Effect Size Estimates' by Gerhart, Wright, McMahan and Snell." *Personnel Psychology* 53 (4):835–45. doi:10.1111/j.1744-6570.2000.tb02419.x.

Katz, H., and I. Darbishire. 2000. *Converging Divergences: Worldwide Changes in Employment Systems*. Ithaca, NY: ILR Press.

Lane, C., and G. Wood. 2009. "Introducing Diversity in Capitalism and Capitalist Diversity." *Economy and Society* 38 (4):531–51. doi:10.1080/03085140903190300.

Lincoln, J., and A. Kalleberg. 1990. *Culture, Control and Commitment: A Study of Work Organization in the United States and Japan*. Cambridge, UK: Cambridge University Press.

Marsden, David, Paul Teague, Enrique M. de la Garza, Wolfgang Streeck, John Pencavel, Kazuo Koike, Harry C. Katz, and Owen Darbishire. 2001. "Change in Employment Systems: Do Common International Trends Imply a Common Destination." *Industrial and Labor Relations Review* 54 (3):682–8.

Mayrhofer, W., and C. Brewster. 2005. "European Human Resource Management: Researching Developments over Time." *Management Revu* 16 (1):36–62. doi:10.5771/0935-9915-2005-1-36.

Mayrhofer, W., C. Brewster, M. J. Morley, and J. Ledolter. 2011. "Hearing a Different Drummer? Evidence of Convergence in European HRM." *Human Resource Management Review* 21 (1):50–67. doi:10.1016/j.hrmr.2010.09.011.

Mayrhofer, W., M. Müller-Camen, J. Ledolter, G. Strunk, and C. Erten. 2002. "The Diffusion of Management Concepts in Europe - Conceptual Considerations and Longitudinal Analysis." *European Journal of Cross-Cultural Competence & Management* 3 (1):315–49.

Moody, K. 1997. *Workers in a Lean World*. London, UK: Verso Books.

Roberts, I. 2003. "Sociology and Industrial Relations." In *Understanding Work and Employment Relations*, edited by P. Ackers and A. Wilkinson, 31–42. Oxford, UK: Oxford University Press.

Streeck, W. 2001. "High Inequality, Low Activity: The Contribution of the Social Welfare System to the German Collective Bargaining Regime." *Industrial and Labor Relations Review* 54 (3):698–706.

Thelen, K. 2001. "Varieties of Labor Politics in the Developed Democracies." In *Varieties of Capitalism: The Institutional Basis of Competitive Advantage*, P. Hall and D. Soskice, edited by 76–92. Oxford, UK: Oxford University Press.

Thelen, K. 2009. "Institutional Change in Advanced Political Economies." *British Journal of Industrial Relations* 47 (3):471–520. doi:10.1111/j.1467-8543.2009.00746.x.

Thelen, K. 2014. *Varieties of Liberalization and the New Politics of Social Solidarity*. Cambridge, UK: Cambridge University Press.

Tregaskis, O., and C. Brewster. 2006. "Converging or Diverging? a Comparative Analysis of Trends in Contingent Employment Practice in Europe over a Decade." *Journal of International Business Studies* 37 (1):111–26. doi:10. 1057/palgrave.jibs.8400174.

Turner, L. 2009. "Institutions and Activism: Crisis and Opportunity for a German Labor Movement in Decline." *ILR Review* 62 (3):294–312. doi:10.1177/001979390906200302.

Walker, J. T., C. Brewster, and G. Wood. 2014. "Diversity between and within Varieties of Capitalism: Transnational Survey Evidence." *Industrial and Corporate Change* 23 (2):493–533. doi:10.1093/icc/dtt014.

Whitley, R. 1999. *Divergent Capitalisms: The Social Structuring and Change of Business Systems.* Oxford, UK: Oxford University Press.

Wilkinson, A., G. T. Wood, and R. Deeg. 2014. *The Oxford Handbook of Employment Relations.* Oxford, UK: Oxford University Press.

Wilthagen, T., and F. Tros. 2004. "The Concept of 'Flexicurity': A New Approach to Regulating Employment and Labour Market *Transfers.*" *European Review of Labour and Research* 10 (2):166–86. doi:10.1177/ 102425890401000204.

Understanding Financial Participation across Market Economies

Elaine Farndale ⓘ, J. Ryan Lamare, Maja Vidović and Amar S. Chauhan

Abstract: Organizations implement a range of financial participation plans to help create a stronger linkage between corporate and individual goals. Although seemingly an organizational-level choice as to what plans are adopted, we argue that institutional constraints at the market economy level of analysis that directly affect worker-firm relationships play a significant role in this choice. Based on organization-level data from nineteen countries, comparisons of the level of profit-sharing and equity-ownership plan use are explained through varieties of capitalism theorizing. The findings indicate the usefulness of this level of analysis in explaining corporate practice in financial participation.

INTRODUCTION

Financial participation is typically viewed as an instrument that motivates employees to work towards the same goals as those of the organization's shareholders, thus alleviating the moral hazard agency problem of firms (Dalton et al. 2007). It has also been looked upon as a form of communication between shareholders and workers (Guery 2013), and can therefore be viewed as an effort to introduce legitimacy about capital (Croucher et al. 2010). In this study, we focus on two forms of financial participation that integrate employer and employee (long-

COMPARATIVE HUMAN RESOURCE MANAGEMENT

and short-term) interests—equity-ownership and profit-sharing. Such plans are widely used by organizations worldwide, and therefore, rather than adopting an individual organizational-level of analysis, we explore here the broader institutional factors that may lead firms to adopt such practices.

Equity-ownership refers to the size of the share in the firm's equity over which the employee has rights, and is implemented through stock option and employee share plans. Such plans are indirectly related to the present value or future profitability of the firm (Poutsma 2001), and imply a long-term relationship with the firm (Braam and Poutsma 2015). Profit-sharing, in contrast, refers to structured plans that give employees a reward that is variable based directly on a firm's result or profitability, which involves allocating a specified percentage of annual profits that is usually dependent on an employee's position in the firm or length of service. Such financial participation plans focus on a shorter-term relationship between employee-employer (Braam and Poutsma 2015). Equity ownership plans incur greater risk for employees due to the uncertain nature of the performance of the firm on the stock markets, whereas profit sharing incurs less risk as there is a more direct relationship with the employee's contribution to the firm (although not unaffected by variables beyond the control of the employee, e.g., rising material costs, fluctuating consumer demand, increasing numbers of profit-sharing participants) (Estrin et al., 1987, 1997).

Financial participation plans are implemented in firms on either a broad-based or restricted basis. Broad-based financial participation plans covering a wide range of employees can facilitate direct participation of workers in the firm (Croucher et al. 2010; Cin, Han, and Smith 2002), yet many profit-sharing and equity-ownership plans are restricted to management-level participation. There are, therefore, choices that firms make in determining whether or not to offer equity-ownership and profit-sharing plans, and to which employees these plans will be offered. However, we argue that such rational choices are constrained by institutional factors that vary across market economies.

Based in varieties of capitalism theorizing (Hall and Soskice 2001), countries can be categorized into different market economies according to patterns of institutional arrangements. Two ideal types of market economy—Liberal Market Economies (LMEs) and Coordinated Market Economies (CMEs)—are most commonly distinguished. While LMEs have a greater focus on corporate autonomy, shareholder wealth, and liberal employment frameworks, CMEs have greater regulation and a focus on a broader group of stakeholders with interests in the firm. In each market economy, business systems theory (Whitley 1999), supported by neo-institutional theory (DiMaggio and Powell 1983), suggest that firms need to achieve legitimacy and they do so by aligning their strategies according to the context (Poutsma, Blasi, and Kruse 2012). As Farndale, Brewster, and Poutsma (2008) demonstrate, significant differences exist in Human Resource Management (HRM) practices, including financial participation, both between firms in LMEs and CMEs, as well as between countries within each type of market economy group.

This LME/CME dichotomy is perhaps, however, too narrow to incorporate the diversity of business systems at a national level. Amable (2003) introduced a more nuanced classification of market economies that includes Continental European (CE), State-Influenced Mediterranean (SIM), Scandinavian Social Democrat (SSD), Asian, and LMEs, based on combinations of institutional factors. Our study contributes to this comparative capitalisms literature by applying Amable's (2003) institutional dimensions per market economy to explore how the different combinations of institutions are associated with the adoption of financial participation plans. Our primary goal is to explore the extent to which the financial participation plans adopted within the firm relate to the market economy institutional constraints on the firm's behavior.

We start with a review of extant literature in which we theorize anticipated relationships between institutional factors and financial participation plan use. Based on these relationships, we hypothesize the relative extent of use of profit-sharing and equity-ownership plans across the different market economies. These hypotheses are tested using the extensive Cranet HRM policies and practices survey data from 2009/10 including 4,253 organization responses from nineteen countries. The detailed findings contribute to the broad varieties of capitalism literature, emphasizing the relevance of this level of analysis for exploring management practice in firms. They also indicate the usefulness of taking an institutional approach to theorizing the adoption of financial participation plans across different market economy contexts, based on the isomorphic effects within market economies (Jackson and Deeg 2008). Building on these findings, ideas for future research in this field are discussed.

FINANCIAL PARTICIPATION

The rationale behind employee financial participation concerns how employees can have active participation in economic aspects of society. In 1958, American lawyer and investment banker, Louis Kelso, proposed a solution to creating employee financial participation opportunities, whereby owners would not be deprived of their property, but non-owners could be incorporated as shareowners (Lowitzsch 2009). Since then, two primary types of financial participation plans for employees have emerged (Poutsma 2001). First, Participation through profit-sharing, structured plans that give employees a reward that is variable based on a firm's results or profitability. Second, Participation through equity-ownership a form of financial participation that is not directly linked with profits but indirectly related to the present value of future profitability. These plans can take the form of equity shares or employee stock options. Usually companies issue these shares from a prescribed quota reserved specifically for employees at a discounted price.

Profit-sharing and equity-ownership plans vary in the risks they carry and how they deliver returns to employees. If an increase in employee productivity results in higher profits, the transfer of benefits to the employees will depend upon whether the company can afford to pay a higher contribution in the profit-sharing plan the following year. Conversely, under equity-ownership, the rise in profits is generally transferred to the employee automatically through a related increase in the firm's stock value, but this increase is only realized when employees sell their equity and when stock markets remain stable. Empirical studies have demonstrated positive links between financial participation and employee productivity (e.g., Kruse and Blasi 1997; McCarthy and Palcic 2012).

Much of the extant financial participation research has focused on studying market economy institutional effects either unilaterally or classifying two broad types of capitalism: LMEs and CMEs (Croucher et al. 2010). Such studies have demonstrated that the use of employee financial participation plans varies less in LME contexts than in CME contexts, as well as there being differences in the use of these plans between foreign-owned multinational enterprises (MNEs), domestic-owned MNEs, and domestic organizations (Farndale, Brewster, and Poutsma 2008). Although useful, this LME/CME dichotomy does not sufficiently reveal the potential differences in institutional drivers within each of these market economies. It is therefore important to develop more nuanced approaches to exploring the use of financial participation plans related to market economy contexts.

Market Economies

Every country has its own set of political-economic institutions that collectively creates the market (or non-market) mechanisms of the country (Ostrom 1986; Höpner 2005). The varieties of capitalism approach, pioneered by Hall and Soskice (2001) and extended further by Amable (2003), is a framework for describing comparative political economies on the basis of strategic interactions between the different institutional players in the economy. Hall and Soskice (2001) classified the developed economies into LMEs and CMEs, the primary difference being whether the economy is guided by market-based mechanisms, such as the LME free market economy of the United States, or a CME non-market coordination mechanism in which different institutions in their markets affect the equilibrium choices (Hall and Soskice 2001; Amable 2003).

There are, however, many markets, such as Italy or Sweden, that are situated in between these two paradigms (Amable 2003). Therefore, to analyze how a firm's financial participation behavior might be affected by its market environment, it is more appropriate to parse the varieties of capitalism into relevant institutional and structural combinations for each characteristic of the economy. Such is the classification of Amable (2003), creating five groupings of economies on the basis of five broad institutional dimensions: product markets, financial markets, Labor markets, social protection, and education systems. We focus here on the first three of these institutions, as these market forces are expected to have the greatest influence on the prevalence of financial participation plans in firms due to their direct effect on worker-firm relationships, as we now describe.

Product markets are the markets in which firms sell their products or services, and vary in the extent to which they can be classified as competitive free-markets, versus regulated markets over which governments exert control (Amable, Ledezma, and Robin 2016). Related to financial participation, product market competition has been found to enhance performance-related pay, stock options (Cuñat and Guadalupe 2004), and incentive-based compensation plans (Beiner, Schmid, and Wanzenried 2011; Funk and Wanzenried 2003): "With greater competition due to increased product substitutability or a larger market, firms provide stronger incentives to their managers to reduce costs, even though profits become more volatile" (Raith 2003, 1432). Shedding more light on this relationship, Beiner, Schmid, and

Wanzenried (2011) found a convex relationship between product market competition and managerial incentive pay: if competition intensity is low, managerial incentive pay will decrease, but under sufficiently high intensity product markets, managerial incentive pay will increase. We therefore propose that competitive markets are likely to show high use of equity-ownership and profit-sharing plans, and that increasing levels of regulation and control will decrease the likelihood of their use.

Financial markets are the markets for the exchange of funds, classified either as market (investor)-based or bank-based (Levine 2002). Financial participation plans have been found to be affected by the dominant financial market structure. For example, a greater proportion of institutional investors (market-based) increases the degree of variable pay for managers while reducing the basic level of compensation (Hartzell and Starks 2003). Stock options also have the "highest sensitivity to a firms' capital structure" (Ortiz-Molina 2007, 21). In LMEs, the financial markets result in short-term pressures from institutional investors for results (Poutsma et al. 2012). We therefore argue that more market-based investment structures (rather than institutionalized financing through banking institutions) will be associated with higher levels of use of equity-ownership and profit-sharing plans. In contrast, where financial markets are less developed, this type of risk is less desirable, resulting in lower use of share ownership and stock options (Jones, Kalmi, and Mäkinen 2006). Long-term financing relationships between firms and banks also indicate low use of stock options (Uchida 2006). As an alternative form of variable pay, we anticipate that profit-sharing plans will also be more prevalent in more investor-focused financial markets.

Labor markets are distinguished by the extent to which employee rights are protected, and workers are represented within firms. High levels of protection and representation are referred to as coordinated labor markets, while liberal labor markets are less regulated to encourage greater competition (Hall and Soskice 2001). With regard to financial participation, high indirect participation has been directly correlated with greater use of profit-sharing (Poutsma, Hendrickx, and Huijgen 2003). Highly regulated labor markets also increase enforced governance and reduce agency cost, thereby allowing companies to spend less on incentive-based pay (Dicks 2012), and wanting to take less risk, avoiding equity ownership plans (Jones, Kalmi, and Mäkinen 2006). Low levels of indirect employee representation, in contrast, are associated with greater use of stock options and share ownership (Poutsma, Kalmi, and Pendleton 2006). Our proposition is therefore that, in more competitive, liberal labor markets with low levels of employee representation, there is greater use of equity-ownership but less use of profit-sharing plans, compared with more regulated labor markets with high levels of employee representation.

Although we do not focus on social protection and education systems in great detail here, as these institutions are expected to have less of a direct effect specifically on financial participation schemes than the three institutions described above, we briefly outline their role in distinguishing market economies. Social protection or national welfare systems evolve from country-specific politics in terms of the extent to which the government allocates social expenditure as a percentage of the gross domestic product (GDP) (Amable 2003). Those countries in which there is a lack of social welfare for workers tend to belong to societies with a greater focus on a free-market economy. With regard to education systems, these can differ based on the extent to which they are differentiated (such as in the United States) or standardized (such as in Germany) (Amable 2003). This determines the extent to which "job-ready" talent is available to employers in any given country.

Critically, Amable (2003) highlights the importance of considering the interaction between these different market institutions, rather than observing any one of them in isolation. Each institution has a different effect on firm-level variables depending on the context formed by its combination with the other institutions (Ostrom 1986; Höpner 2005). For example, the structure of education in a country, and hence the related need for organizations to offer training, should be considered along with a firm's relationship with banks, because there may be interaction effects on levels of investment in training: Popov's (2014) survey of 8,265 firms found that availability of bank credit affects a firm's investment in on-the-job training, with a 15 percent drop in the probability of training being provided by a firm that is credit constrained.

Amable (2003) further explains how one institution can affect the working of another. For instance, a company's relationship with its creditors can promote long-term investment, thereby providing the opportunity to stimulate stable labor relations. Furthermore, studying a firm's response strategy in light of a single institution, while holding others constant, may not help in understanding clearly the effect of that institution on the firm's actions. For example, it has previously been assumed that centralized bargaining would lead to higher wages, but research has demonstrated an inverted U-shaped relationship whereby totally market-based or totally coordinated structures will both put constraints on wages (Calmfors et al. 1988).

As a result of combining these institutional dimensions in different country groupings, Amable (2003) identified five different market economies. We explore each of these market economies and their institutions in turn to uncover the usefulness of the varieties of capitalism level of analysis in explaining corporate practice in financial participation.

LINKING FINANCIAL PARTICIPATION PLANS WITH MARKET ECONOMIES

Taking each market economy in turn, we develop arguments based on institutional reasoning regarding the prevalence of profit-sharing and equity-ownership financial participation plans. We conclude this section stating two hypotheses designed to test the overall use of these two forms of financial participation across different market economies, i.e. identifying the market economies in which we expect each form to be most or least prevalent. Table 1 summarizes this argumentation, matching the three institutional dimensions to the five market economies, and indicating anticipated levels of use of profit-sharing and equity-ownership plans.

Continental Europe

This market economy includes Germany, France, Austria, Belgium, Norway, The Netherlands, and Switzerland (Amable 2003). Product markets are regulated to an average extent according to the Organisation for Economic Co-operation and Development (OECD) norms, except for in the Netherlands where they are somewhat more competitive (OECD

TABLE 1

Core Institutional Characteristics of Five Market Economies Linked to the Use of Financial
Participation Plans

	Continental European	State-Influenced Mediterranean	Scandinavian Social Democrat	Asian	Liberal Market Economy
Product markets	Medium regulation	High regulation	Medium to low regulation	Very high regulation	Competitive
Financial markets	Bank/market-based	Bank-based	Bank-based	Bank-based	Market-based
Labor markets	Coordinated (some competition)	Coordinated (emphasis on role of government)	Coordinated (emphasis on role of trade unions)	Coordinated (emphasis on long-term welfare of employees)	Liberal/competitive
Hypothesized use of equity-ownership plans	Medium *3rd Most prevalent*	Low *Least prevalent*	Medium-low *4th Most prevalent*	Medium-high *2nd Most prevalent*	High *Most prevalent*
Hypothesized use of profit-sharing plans	Medium-high *Joint most prevalent*	Low *Least prevalent*	Medium *Joint 2nd most prevalent*	Medium-high *Joint most prevalent*	Medium *Joint 2nd most prevalent*

2015). Financial markets are dominated by banks that have major stakes in corporations with long-term credit-based relationships with firms. Yet at the same time, stock markets are highly developed, also creating market-based demands (Amable 2003). Although the labor markets are competitive with skilled and organized workforces (Poutsma, Hendrickx, and Huijgen 2003), there is substantial coordination and protection provided in the workplace through a high degree of indirect employee representation and protection. Employees have leverage through strong trade union influence in bargaining, which is usually organized at the industry level with some room for flexibility at the company level (Amable 2003; Hall and Soskice 2001). Industrial relations are based on cooperation rather than conflict, with an emphasis on a stakeholder approach to corporate governance (Almond, Edwards, and Clark 2003).

Based on these institutional characteristics, we anticipate greater use of profit-sharing plans than equity-ownership plans due to average levels of product market regulation, the mix of bank-based and market-based financing, and a dominance of indirect representation and wage bargaining structures. Legislation and tax incentives to promote profit-sharing are also dominant in one country in this market economy: France (Estrin et al. 1997). As the financial market relationship between firms and banks is generally more long-term rather than demanding quick returns, firms will be less in favor of taking risks such as those associated with share ownership and stock options. Equity-ownership use is nevertheless anticipated to be at a medium (average) level relative to the other market economies, as there are highly developed stock markets.

State-Influenced Mediterranean

This market economy includes Spain, Portugal, Greece, and Italy (Amable 2003). These countries are characterized by increasingly high regulation of product markets, with Greece having one of the highest levels of administrative market regulation (OECD 2015). The economies' financial markets depend minimally on market-based mechanisms, and have low percentages of institutional investors compared to banks, pension funds, and insurance companies (Amable 2003). The OECD ranked these economies as having the strictest regulation of employment protection within the European Union (OECD 2009), with strong government influence on employment regulations (Schmidt 2007). The relationship between management and worker representation is typically conflict-based (Romo 2005).

In this market economy, we expect to see the lowest levels of market-based plans in the financial participation portfolio. As product markets are increasingly regulated and financial markets remain underdeveloped as a result of state intervention, financial participation plans are anticipated to be less related to market-based risk, resulting in low use of equity-ownership plans. Although there is high indirect participation (normally directly correlated with profit-sharing), there has been substantive evidence for a decrease in performance-based pay incentives under high government regulation (Perry and Zenner 2001). We therefore expect the lowest levels of both profit-sharing and equity-ownership plans in this market economy relative to the other market economies.

Scandinavian Social Democrat

Sweden, Denmark, and Finland are the countries that form this market economy (Amable, 2003). A notable feature of these market economies is the close to average but lower degree of regulation of product markets compared to the CE and SIM models (Amable 2003). Financial markets are dominated by companies having access to patient capital through banks, meaning that credit availability is not always tied to profits (Hall and Soskice 2001). These three economies follow a social democratic structure in the labor market, evidenced by high trade union membership levels and highly centralized collective bargaining coverage (ETUI 2015). The result is highly coordinated labor markets, in which trade unions play a significant role.

Based on the medium-to-low regulation of product markets, bank-based financing, and high indirect participation and coordination of the labor market, we expect to see medium (average) levels of financial participation based on both profit-sharing and equity-ownership plans, relative to the other market economies. Specifically, due to the lower regulation of product markets than in CE, we might expect higher use of equity-ownership in SSD, yet the financial markets are more purely bank-focused than in CE, indicating less use of equity-ownership. Combined with the greater level of labor market coordination than CE, overall, we expect lower levels overall in SSD of equity-ownership than in CE.

Asian

Japan and South Korea combine to form this Asian market economy (Amable 2003). Product markets are distinct from CE, SIM, or SSD economies, in that they are very strongly regulated (Amable 2003). Economic policy is adopted to balance state intervention and free market demands, with the state being more inclined to protect successful domestic firms from foreign competition (Cerny 2005). South Korea is cited as a marked example of economic success that implemented this model, which notably failed in India (Chibber 2003). The financial market's relationship with the firm is credit-based and has a long-term objective, with firms predominantly being financed through banking institutions (Uchida 2006). These countries have highly coordinated labor markets where a top priority is protection of employment (Amable 2003). A further distinction of this model, especially in Japan, is an inbuilt lack of social security and indirect dependence on companies (Cho 1996), whereby care for the long-term welfare of employees is an important institutional feature.

These institutional factors (very highly regulated product markets, bank-based financial markets, and highly coordinated labor markets) lead us to believe that the regulated product markets will somewhat constrain the use of stock options. Given also the long-term financing relationship between firms and banks, this would also indicate low use of stock options. Since the Asian financial crisis in the late 1990s, however, dynamics are said to have changed, with firms increasingly inclined to use stock options to align with North American "best practice" in financial participation (Ahmadijan 2001). We therefore anticipate a medium (average) to high use of equity-ownership plans relative to the other market economies. Given the highly regulated labor market context and systems of indirect worker participation, we also expect to see medium (average) to high use of profit-sharing plans.

Liberal Market Economies

This final market economy includes the Anglo-Saxon countries of the USA, UK, Australia and Canada (Amable 2003). LMEs are characterized by competitive product markets with very limited levels of regulation (Amable 2003; OECD 2015). Financial markets are well developed, and the importance of institutional investors is realized. Firms seek to maximize shareholder value in the wake of a threat of takeover if they do not follow that objective (Grant 2010). Relationships between investors and firms are built on short-term profits (Hall and Soskice 2001), encouraging the use of incentive plans to motivate employee performance. Labor market policies are very liberal, allowing firm autonomy (Farndale, Brewster, and Poutsma 2008). This results in a competitive labor market that is less influenced by third-parties and more open to free-market forces. Indirect employee representation is less common than in other models of capitalism (Almond, Edwards, and Clark 2003).

Based on these institutional factors, we expect the highest use of stock options and share ownership, encouraged by low levels of indirect employee representation and labor market regulation. Given that product markets are competitive, there are highly developed financial markets with investor-firm relationships leveraged on short-term profits, and there is the highest emphasis on maximizing shareholder value, equity-ownership plans are expected to be used more commonly than in any of the other market economies discussed here. With the indirect participation rate being lower, however, we expect to see a medium (average) use of profit-sharing plans.

Hypotheses

As summarized in Table 1, although it is expected that both equity-ownership and profit-sharing financial participation plans will be used in all five market economies, based on the preceding theorizing, we offer the following two hypotheses:

TABLE 2
Respondents

Market economy	Number of respondents	Respondents per country
Continental European	1,333	Austria = 203
		Belgium = 240
		France = 157
		Germany = 420
		Netherlands = 116
		Norway = 98
		Switzerland = 99
State-Influenced Mediterranean	371	Greece = 214
		Italy = 157
Scandinavian Social Democrat	780	Denmark = 362
		Finland = 136
		Sweden = 282
Asian Model	389	Japan = 389
Liberal Market Economy	1,380	UK = 218
		USA = 1,052
		Australia = 110
Total	4,253	

Data was not available from Spain and Portugal (SIM), South Korea (Asian), and Canada (LME).

H1: Financial participation plans based on equity-ownership will be most prevalent in LMEs, followed first by Asian, then by CE, and then by SSD market economies, and least prevalent in SIM market economies.

H2: Financial participation plans based on profit-sharing will be most prevalent in both CE and Asian market economies, followed first by SSD and LMEs, and least prevalent in SIM market economies.

METHODOLOGY

The hypotheses are tested using 2009/10 Cranet data from nineteen countries representing the five market economy models ($n = 4,253$) (see Table 2). The Cranet survey aims to draw representative national samples across multiple countries. Data are collected from full population surveys in many countries and from representative random samples in the larger countries. The questionnaire is designed by an international team in English and then translated and back-translated (Brislin 1976) into the language or languages of each country. The survey is targeted at senior-level managers responsible for HRM. These managers are selected as key informants as they are likely to be well-versed in the firm's financial participation plans. In the survey, HR managers were asked to respond to "yes/no" questions as to whether they used employee share schemes and/or stock options (equity-based plans), and profit- sharing plans, separately for four employee levels—management, technical/professional, clerical, and manual.

Control Variables

Several control variables are applied to accommodate for different organizational determinants in addition to the effect of market economy based on extant literature. First, firms are likely to use financial participation schemes when they are expected to have a positive impact on their profit-seeking activities. For example, Kalmi, Pendleton, and Poutsma's (2005) study of 209 listed firms from the UK, Netherlands, Germany, and Finland found that equity-based ownership is positively related to productivity, while profit-sharing does not have a similar effect or any complementary relationship with other forms of participation. This is contradictory to the normally-held belief that financial participation works best with other forms of participation. They attribute the reason for this to the fact that firms in their study were publicly listed, whereby a sense of ownership is less important and any financial participation schemes are seen as "supplementary" rewards. We measure this control by including two variables: a dummy variable for whether the firm is publicly listed (62.5% of firms did not report being publicly listed); and dummy variables for whether the firm was reporting its profit over the previous three years as being high, modest, enough to break even, insufficient to cover costs, or leading to large losses (12.1% of firms fell into the top two categories, and 33.8% into the bottom two).

Second, the extent to which a firm has formal mechanisms of employee representation may determine its use of financial participation plans. Our reasoning lies in the difference between stakeholder and shareholder models of corporate governance, whereby the former is known for its greater employee representation. While shareholder firms aim to maximize equity value, stakeholder firms have broader objectives that consider added value to all parties who have a stake in the organization (Jones et al. 2012; Tirole 2001). Research shows that the recent trend towards the shareholder approach in countries such as Finland has contributed to increased use of participation schemes (Jones et al. 2012; Poutsma and De Nijs 2003). However, it is also argued that because stakeholder firms have less pressure to maximize short-term profit, they can therefore share rewards with their workers (Blair 1995; Levine 1995). In order to measure the extent of stakeholder (rather than shareholder) influence, we include two proxy variables typically evident in stakeholder model firms: the level of influence of trade unions (scaled 1–5, where 1 = no union influence at all, and 5 = a very great extent of union influence); and the presence of work councils (66.6% of firms reported having a works council).

Third, a firm's age and size have been found to be significant predictors of financial participation plan use (Lavelle et al. 2012). For example, new firms need to expend more effort in aligning the long-term interests of employees with their own than established firms. They are also expected to have equity-based plans rather than profit-sharing, as early year profits are less likely (Lavelle et al. 2012; Pendleton et al. 2001). The link between firm size and financial participation is less predictable but nevertheless evident, dependent to some extent on the anticipated benefits of using financial participation to counter the effects of power inequalities as firms increase in size (Lavelle et al. 2012). Firm age and the number of employees are therefore included in the analysis.

TABLE 3
Percentage of Firms using Financial Participation Plans by Employee Level

	Management	Professional/Technical	Clerical	Manual
Employee share scheme	21.9	14.9	13.8	10.9
Stock options	18.3	7.8	5.2	3.0
Profit sharing scheme	28.8	23.5	20.1	14.4

Finally, the level of capital intensity of a firm has been found to be related to plan use, whereby high intensity is associated with the highest need for firms to align the interests of managers and workers with corporate objectives (Lavelle et al. 2012). We use a proxy measure of capital intensity based on whether the firm is in the manufacturing sector (indicating high capital intensity) rather than the services sector (64.9% of firms reported being in manufacturing).

In summary, these firm characteristics (public listing, profitability, trade union influence, works council presence, firm age, number of employees, capital intensity) are included in the analyses as control variables to consider other potential explanations for variance in financial participation plan use.

RESULTS

To analyze financial participation plan use, we calculate the plan incidence for each employee type within a firm. This helps explore the effects of market economy and types of employees using a logit regression model incorporating company fixed-effects as each unit of observation is repeated for each type of employee. In other words, for each firm the dependent variable is whether the scheme, which is being regressed on the explanatory variables, is offered (coded as 1) or not (coded as 0). For each scheme, it is recorded whether or not the scheme is offered to each of the four employees levels: management, professional/technical, clerical, and manual.

Table 3 presents the percentage of firms reporting the use of financial participation plans by employee level. It shows that all plans are used across employee levels, although with decreasing frequency as the level decreases (as expected). It is noteworthy that there is a particularly noticeable decrease in use from managers to the lower levels for stock options.

The independent variable in the analysis is market economy, designated as CE, SSD, SIM, Asian, or LME. We fit the following model to our data, where Y_i is a binary measure of each of the three financial participation plans (share schemes, stock options, and profit-sharing):

$$Y_i = \beta_0 + \beta_1 \text{Market Economy} + \beta_2 \text{Employee Type} + \beta_3 \text{Controls} + \beta_4 \text{Firm Fixed Effects} + \varepsilon_i.$$

TABLE 4
Logit Regression Coefficients for Financial Participation Plan Use

Dependent variable	Employee share scheme	Stock options	Profit sharing
Scandinavian Social Democrat	−0.08	−1.34*	−3.64***
	(0.72)	(0.65)	(0.56)
State-Influenced Mediterranean	−0.82	1.81**	−6.18***
	(0.72)	(0.56)	(0.62)
Liberal Market Economy	1.24*	2.41***	−1.74**
	(0.68)	(0.59)	(0.54)
Asian	7.54***	−0.41	−5.92***
	(0.29)	(0.60)	(0.65)
Professional/Technical	−3.14***	−3.30***	−1.13***
	(0.29)	(0.27)	(0.15)
Clerical	−3.48***	−4.81***	−1.87***
	(0.31)	(0.36)	(0.17)
Manual	−4.95***	−6.11***	−3.68***
	(0.40)	(0.46)	(0.22)
Number of employees	0.00	−0.00	0.00
	(0.00)	(0.00)	(0.00)
Union influence (small)	0.31	−0.89**	0.49
	(0.57)	(0.92)	(0.50)
Union influence (moderate)	0.06	−0.17	1.15*
	(0.62)	(0.78)	(0.52)
Union influence (great)	−0.62	−1.03	0.91
	(0.85)	(0.60)	(0.63)
Union influence (very great)	−2.67	0.22	−0.07
	(1.64)	(0.43)	(1.37)
Works council presence	1.46**	1.02*	−0.23
	(0.5)	(0.46)	(0.43)
Public listing	5.01***	4.82***	0.24
	(0.47)	(0.50)	(0.35)
Capital intensity (manufacturing)	−0.44	0.19	−1.20***
	(0.42)	(0.38)	(0.35)
Firm age	−0.00	0.00	0.00
	(0.00)	(0.00)	(0.00)
Profit (modest profit)	−1.04	1.99*	1.13
	(1.53)	(0.86)	(.90)
Profit (breakeven)	2.02	0.00	0.91
	(1.32)	(0.70)	(0.77)
Profit (costs not covered)	−3.04**	−0.283	−0.25
	(1.03)	(0.54)	(0.57)
Profit (large losses)	1.85**	−0.19	−0.11
	(0.66)	(0.38)	(0.38)
AIC	2,897.8	2,572.0	4,168.2
BIC	3,046.1	2,720.3	4,316.5
Log Likelihood	−1,426.9	−1,264.0	−2,062.1
No. of observations	6,253	6,225	6,263
No. of groups: Firm	1,596	1,598	1,601
Variance: Firm (Intercept)	30.97	22.5	27.43
Residual	1.00	1.00	1.00

Standard error in parentheses.
***$p < 0.001$, **$p < 0.01$, *$p < 0.05$.

In each model, the reference category (for categorical variables) is the CE market economy as this is the largest group, and the management employee level as this represents the group most likely to be included. Table 4 shows the results of the logit regression.

For employee share schemes, supporting our initial descriptive results, employee share schemes are used most for management and least for manual employees ($\beta = -4.95$; se $= 0.40$; $p < 0.001$). The presence of work councils, publicly listed firms, and firms operating with low profitability are also significantly ($p < 0.01$) and positively related to the use of employee share schemes. Testing hypothesis 1, we found that SSD ($\beta = -0.08$; se $= 0.72$) and SIM ($\beta = -0.82$; se $= 0.72$) firms do not differ from the CE reference category, but LME ($\beta = 1.24$; se $= 0.78$; $p < 0.05$) and Asian ($\beta = 7.54$; se $= 0.29$; $p < 0.001$) firms are significantly more likely to provide these schemes. We also tested for the significance of the coefficient differences across the market economies (rather than the reference group). For this, we used a simultaneous test within a general linear hypothesis. Since this is a multiple hypothesis, we therefore avoid the multiple comparison problem by using the Bonferroni correction. The results of this test show that only the Asian market economy has a significantly different coefficient from the other four market economies. This second test largely confirms the initial findings, with the only point of difference being the ranking of LME firms.

For stock options, stock options are least likely to be offered to manual employees ($\beta = -6.11$; se $= 0.46$; $p < 0.001$) and most likely for management employees. Finally, being publicly listed ($p < 0.001$) and making modest profits ($p < 0.05$) are significantly positively associated with stock option use. Testing hypothesis 1 further, stock options are more likely to be used in LME ($\beta = 2.41$; se $= 0.59$; $p < 0.001$) and SIM ($\beta = 1.81$; se $= 0.56$; $p < 0.01$) market economies relative to the CE reference category, while they are less likely to occur in SSD ($\beta = -1.34$; se $= 0.65$; $p < 0.05$) firms. There is no significant difference between Asian firms ($\beta = -0.41$; se $= 0.60$) and the CE reference category. When testing for the significance of the coefficient differences across the market economies, the effect of CE firms is not different from SSD and Asia firms, nor is the effect of SIM firms different from that of LME firms. Again, the second test largely confirms the first, with only SSD firms being classified differently.

Overall with regard to hypothesis 1, for both employee share schemes and stock options (equity ownership), we anticipated these to be used most in LME, followed by Asian, then CE, and then SSD firms, and least in SIM firms. For share schemes, this is partially supported as LME and Asian firms were found to use this practice most, while CE, SSD, and SIM firms use share schemes least. For stock options, the pattern is slightly different: LME and (unexpectedly) SIM show the most common use, whereas the lowest use is in CE, SSD, and (unexpectedly) Asia firms.

For profit-sharing, again confirming the descriptive findings, these schemes are least common for manual employees ($\beta = -3.68$; se $= 0.22$; $p < 0.001$) and most common for management. Finally, high capital intensity firms are significantly ($p < 0.001$) less likely to use profit-sharing, while firms with moderate union influence are significantly ($p < 0.05$) more likely to use this practice. Testing hypothesis 2, we find that SIM ($\beta = -6.18$; se $= 0.62$; $p < 0.001$), Asian ($\beta = -5.92$; se $= 0.65$; $p < 0.001$), SSD ($\beta = -3.64$; se $= 0.56$; $p < 0.001$), and LME ($\beta = -1.74$; se $= 0.54$; $p < 0.01$) firms are all significantly different from the CE reference group, with each region being less likely to offer profit sharing than firms from CE. When testing for the significance of the coefficient differences across the market economies, however, the effects of SIM and Asian firms are not statistically different from each other (though they do differ relative to CE firms). Similarly, the effects of LME firms are not significantly different from CE or SSD market economies.

With regard to hypothesis 2, we anticipated profit-sharing would be used most in CE and Asian firms, followed by SSD, and LME firms, and least in SIM firms. There is again partial support, as CE firms do show the highest level of use and SIM firms the lowest level of use. However, Asian firms show a low level of use rather than high as expected.

DISCUSSION

Financial participation plans represent a set of management practices that firms can largely choose to implement (other than where this is mandated by law, e.g., in France; Estrin et al. 1997), with the expectation that they will help to motivate employees to improve the bottom-line performance of the firm (Dalton et al. 2007). The extent to which such plans are put in place has previously been found to be associated with such characteristics as firm size, age and capital intensity (Lavelle et al. 2012), whether a firm is publicly listed (Kalmi, Pendleton, and Poutsma 2005), and the extent of the firm's stakeholder rather than share-holder corporate governance model (Jones et al. 2012). The study presented here has expanded upon this organization-level of analysis, exploring the extent to which institutional factors at market economy level can be applied as explanatory variables for financial participation use.

Taking employee share schemes and stock options as examples of long-term equity-based financial participation plans, these are contrasted with the shorter-term profit-sharing plans (Braam and Poutsma 2015). Based on Amable's (2003) classification of countries into five market economies (CE, SIM, SSD, Asian, and LME), their typical product, financial, and labor market characteristics were used to characterize each market economy, proposing how these factors might influence short and long-term financial participation plan use. As Table 1 summarized, it was proposed that high regulation of product markets and strong control of financial markets were likely to combine to reduce the incidence of both equity-based and profit-sharing plans due to their inherent levels of risk (Jones et al. 2006; Raith 2003). In contrast, strong coordination of labor markets was likely to increase the use of profit-sharing but decrease the incidence of equity-based plans based on patterns of employee representation (Poutsma, Hendrickx, and Huijgen 2003).

This institutional reasoning was applied to the five market economies, developing two hypotheses comparing anticipated levels of use of the different financial participation plans. These hypotheses received some support, highlighting how market economies differ significantly in their use of financial participation plans. For example, while SIM firms were found to show low use of employee share schemes and profit-sharing, LME firms were high in the use of equity-based plans but lower in the use of profit-sharing. We consider the implications of these findings further here.

In LME countries, the competitive, market-based product, and financial markets, combined with a relatively low level of labor market regulation mean that financial participation might be used to motivate employees to work towards the same goals as those of the firm's shareholders. In contrast, in SIM, the combination of highly regulated product markets and underdeveloped competitive financial markets, combined with an unwillingness to take risk mean that the context is not conducive for the use of financial participation plans. The only unexpected finding here was the relatively high use of stock options in SIM firms, which does not fit the institutional profile. Despite evidence of a decline in the use of performance-based pay incentives under high government regulation (Perry and Zenner 2001), stock options appear to be of interest to firms in these countries. Future qualitative research could be interesting to undertake in exploring why.

The CE countries hold a middle position between the SIM and LME contexts, with moderate levels of product market regulation, a balance between market-based and bank-dominated financial markets, and labor markets that are largely coordinated but with competitive elements. Their use of equity-based financial participation plans was also around the mid-level comparing across the market economies, while the use of profit-sharing was relatively high, as expected. Balancing the levels of regulation with free-market forces results in greater use of employee share ownership and profit-sharing plans than in SIM countries, though somewhat less than in the much freer markets of LME. A similar situation was observed in the SSD countries, but with slightly lower use of equity-based and profit-sharing compared to CE countries. Lower levels of product market regulation appear to be balanced against a less free-market approach to finance to result in mid-levels of financial participation plans.

There were, however, other unanticipated results. The discrepancy between anticipated and observed use of financial participation plans was primarily evident for the Asian firms (for stock options and profit-sharing). One reason for this finding may be that the Asian market economy in the analysis only included firms in Japan as the data were not available for South Korea. South Korea has been identified as a strong example of balancing state intervention and free-market demands (Chibber 2003), whereas Japan places greater emphasis on companies to support long-term employee welfare due to its lack of social security (Cho 1996). This greater reliance on the corporate world may mean that the product, financial, and labor markets operate differently from those in South Korea, leading to the observed lower use of profit-sharing and stock options than anticipated. Further research on specific country-level institutional factors that affect worker-firm relationships could help to clarify this finding.

Overall, the findings indicate that product, financial, and labor market factors can be considered as institutional constraints to corporate agency in selecting whether or not to implement financial participation plans. By adopting Amable's (2003) distinction between five different types of market economy, this level of analysis enabled us to contribute to our understanding of financial participation use. We have demonstrated that such plans are a product of economic, regulatory, and market factors operating in the macro context of firms, influencing management practice. As such, these findings provide further evidence of isomorphism within market economies: Different market economies are expected to have different patterns of management practice adoption and diffusion based on "systematically interdependent configurations" (Jackson and Deeg 2008, 545). Future research can continue to benefit from the relevance market economy level of analysis in investigating financial participation plan use.

CONCLUSIONS

This study has explored whether a firm's financial participation practices are related to the institutional configurations of the market economy in which it operates. Based on institutional theorizing, we anticipated a certain ranking in the use of both equity-ownership and profit-sharing financial participation plans. The study's findings largely support the anticipated associations between institutional factors and the use of financial participation plans. The differences between market economies in the use of equity-based and profit-sharing plans have been highlighted. Future research can now explore further how these differences manifest themselves in creating systems of employee financial participation.

Despite these interesting findings, the study is, of course, subject to certain limitations, the first of which is that the data only record whether or not the various financial participation plans are offered to employees, rather than exploring the extent to which they are taken up by employees. As noted, a further limitation of this study is that limited data were available, with not all countries being represented in each market economy, with for example, Japan being the sole representative of the Asian model. The addition of further countries in future research would be a valuable contribution to knowledge in this field.

On the basis of this study, it is clear that the market economy level of analysis is an important variable in explaining financial participation plan use across market economies, in addition to extant organizational and country-level studies. For practice, this means that MNEs operating across market economies should consider these institutional constraints (product, financial, and labor markets) when implementing financial participation practices. We look forward to observing how future research might extend the findings presented here both to additional forms of financial participation, and to an even broader range of market economy countries.

ORCID

Elaine Farndale (iD) http://orcid.org/0000-0001-5871-5840

REFERENCES

Ahmadjian, C. 2001. "Changing Japanese Corporate Governance" Working paper No. 188, Center on Japanese Economy and Business, Columbia Business School.

Almond, P., T. Edwards, and I. Clark. 2003. "Multinationals and Changing National Business Systems in Europe: Towards the 'Shareholder Value' Model?" *Industrial Relations Journal* 34 (5):430–45. doi:10.1111/j.1468-2338. 2003.00288.x.

Amable, B. 2003. *The Diversity of Modern Capitalism*. New York, NY: Oxford University Press.

Amable, B., I. Ledezma, and S. Robin. 2016. "Product Market Regulation, Innovation and Productivity." *Research Policy* 45 (10):2087–104. doi:10.1016/j.respol.2016.08.003

Beiner, S., M. M. Schmid, and G. Wanzenried. 2011. "Product Market Competition, Managerial Incentives and Firm Valuation." *European Financial Management* 17 (2):331–66. doi:10.1111/j.1468-036X.2009.00505.x.

Blair, M. M. 1995. *Ownership and Control: Rethinking Corporate Governance for the Twenty-First Century*. Washington, DC: Brookings Institution Press.

Braam, G., and E. Poutsma. 2015. "Broad-Based Financial Participation Plans and Their Impact on Financial Performance: Evidence from a Dutch Longitudinal Panel." *De Economist* 163 (2):177–202. doi:10.1007/s10645-014-9249-1.

Brislin, R. W. (Ed.) 1976. *Translation: Applications and Research*. New York, NY: Wiley.

Calmfors, L., J. Driffill, S. Honkapohja, and F. Giavazzi. 1988. "Bargaining Structure, Corporatism and Macroeconomic Performance." *Economic Policy* 3 (6), 13. Reprinted in *The Economics of Unemployment*, ed. P.N. Junankar, Vol. III, Edward Elgar, 2000.

Cerny, P. 2005. "Power, Markets and Authority: The Development of Multi-level Governance in International Finance." In *Governing Financial Globalization*, edited by Baker, A., A. Hudson and R. Woodward. New York, NY: Routledge.

Chibber, V. 2003. *Locked in Place: State-Building and LateIindustrialization in India*. Princeton, NJ: Princeton University Press. doi:10.1086/ahr/109.4.1214.

Cho, Y.-H. 1996. "The Growth of Enterprise Welfare in Japan." *Economic and Industrial Democracy* 17 (2): 281–300. doi:10.1177/0143831X96172006.

Cin, B., T. Han, and S. Smith. 2002. "A Tale of Two Tigers: Employee Financial Participation in Taiwan and Korea." *The International Journal of Human Resource Management* 14 (6):920–41. doi:10.1080/0958519032000106146.

Croucher, R., M. Brookes, G. Wood, and C. Brewster. 2010. "Context, Strategy and Financial Participation: A Comparative Analysis." *Human Relations* 63 (6):835–55. doi:10.1177/0018726709343654.

Cuñat, V., and M. Guadalupe. 2004. *Executive Compensation and Product Market Competition*. Centre for Economic Performance. London: London School of Economics and Political Science.

Dalton, D. R., M. A. Hitt, S. T. Certo, and C. M. Dalton. 2007. "Chapter 1: The Fundamental Agency Problem and Its Mitigation." *The Academy of Management Annals* 1 (1):1–64. doi:10.1080/078559806.

Dicks, D. L. 2012. "Executive Compensation and the Role for Corporate Governance Regulation." *Review of Financial Studies* 25 (6):1971–2004. doi:10.1093/rfs/hhs055.

DiMaggio, P. J., and W. W. Powell. 1983. "The Iron Cage Revisited: Institutional Isomorphism and Collective Rationality in Organizational Fields." *American Sociological Review* 48 (2):147–60. doi:10.2307/2095101.

Estrin, Saul, Paul Grout, Sushil Wadhwani, S. J. Nickell, and Mervyn King. 1987. "Profit-Sharing and Employee Share Ownership." *Economic Policy* 2 (4):13–52. doi:10.2307/1344552.

Estrin, S., V. Perotin, A. Robinson, and N. Wilson. 1997. "Profit-Sharing in OECD Countries: A Review and Some Evidence." *Business Strategy Review* 8 (4):27–32. doi:10.1111/1467-8616.00045.

ETUI. 2015. "Collective Bargaining." Accessed October 8, 2015: http://www.worker-participation.eu/National-Industrial-Relations/Across-Europe/Collective-Bargaining2.

Farndale, E., C. Brewster, and E. Poutsma. 2008. "Coordinated vs. Liberal Market HRM: The Impact of Institutionalization on Multinational Firms." *The International Journal of Human Resource Management* 19 (11): 2004–23. doi:10.1080/09585190802404247.

Funk, P., and G. Wanzenried. 2003. "Product Market Competition and Executive Compensation: An Empirical Investigation." Working Paper No. 03.09, Department of Economics, University of Bern.

Grant, R. M. 2010. *Contemporary Strategy Analysis*. Chichester: John Wiley & Sons.

Guery, L. 2013. "Safeguarding Investments in Human Capital: Evidence of Complementarity between ESO and Involvement Practices." Paper presented at 25th Annual Conference of SASE (Society for the Advancement of Socio-Economics), Milan, Italy, June 27–29.

Hall, P., and D. Soskice. 2001. *Varieties of Capitalism: The Institutional Basis of Competitive Advantage*. Oxford, UK: Oxford University Press.

Hartzell, J. C., and L. T. Starks. 2003. "Institutional Investors and Executive Compensation." *The Journal of Finance* 58 (6):2351–74. doi:10.1046/j.1540-6261.2003.00608.x.

Höpner, M. 2005. "What Connects Industrial Relations and Corporate Governance? Explaining Institutional Complementarity." *Socio-Economic Review* 3 (2):331–58.

Jackson, G., and R. Deeg. 2008. "Comparing Capitalisms: Understanding Institutional Diversity and Its Implication for International Business." *Journal of International Business Studies* 39 (4):540–61. doi:10.1057/palgrave.jibs. 8400375.

Jones, D. C., P. Kalmi, and M. Mäkinen. 2006. "The Determinants of Stock Option Compensation: Evidence from Finland." *Industrial Relations* 45 (3):437–68. doi:10.1111/j.1468-232X.2006.00432.x.

Jones, D. C., P. Kalmi, T. Kato, and M. Mäkinen. 2012. "Financial Participation in Finland: Incidence and Determinants." *The International Journal of Human Resource Management* 23 (8):1570–89. doi:10.1080/ 09585192.2012.661990.

Kalmi, P., A. Pendleton, and E. Poutsma. 2005. "Financial Participation and Performance in Europe." *Human Resource Management Journal* 15 (4):54–67. doi:10.1111/j.1748-8583.2005.tb00295.x.

Kruse, D., and J. Blasi. 1997. "Employee Ownership, Employee Attitudes, and Firm Performance." In *Handbook of Resource Management*, edited by D. J. B. Mitchell, D. Lewin, and M. Zaidi, 113–51. Greenwich, CT: JAI Press.

Lavelle, J., T. Turner, P. Gunnigle, and A. McDonnell. 2012. "The Determinants of Financial Participation Schemes within Multinational Companies in Ireland." *The International Journal of Human Resource Management* 23 (8): 1590–610. doi:10.1080/09585192.2012.661991.

Levine, R. 2002. *Bank-Based or Market-Based Financial Systems: Which Is Better?* Cambridge, MA: National Bureau of Economic Research Inc.

Levine, D. I. 1995. *Reinventing the Workplace: How Business and Employees Can Both Win.* Washington, DC: Brookings Institution Press.

Lowitzsch, J. 2009. *Financial Participation of Employees in the EU-27.* New York, NY: Palgrave Macmillan.

McCarthy, D., and D. Palcic. 2012. "The Impact of Largescale Employee Share Ownership Plans on Labour Productivity: The Case of Eircom." *The International Journal of Human Resource Management* 23 (17): 3710–24. doi:10.1080/09585192.2012.655762.

OECD. 2009. "OECD Indicators of Employment Protection Legislation." Accessed October 7, 2015. http://www. oecd.org/employment/emp/oecdindicatorsofemploymentprotection.htm.

OECD. 2015. "OECD Indicators of Product Market Regulation." Accessed October 8, 2015. http://www.oecd.org/ eco/reform/indicatorsofproductmarketregulationhomepage.htm.

Ortiz-Molina, H. 2007. "Executive Compensation and Capital Structure: The Effects of Convertible Debt and Straight Debt on CEO Pay." *Journal of Accounting and Economics* 43 (1):69–93. doi:10.1016/j.jacceco.2006.09. 003.

Ostrom, E. 1986. "An Agenda for the Study of Institutions." *Public Choice* 48 (1):3–25. doi:10.1007/BF00239556.

Pendleton, A., E. Poutsma, C. Brewster, and J. Van Ommeren. 2001. *Employee Share Ownership and Profit-Sharing in the European Union.* Dublin, Ireland: European Foundation for the Improvement of Living and Working Conditions.

Perry, T., and M. Zenner. 2001. "Pay for Performance? Government Regulation and the Structure of Compensation Contracts." *Journal of Financial Economics* 62 (3):453–88. doi:10.1016/S0304-405X(01)00083-6.

Popov, A. 2014. "Credit Constraints and Investment in Human Capital: Training Evidence from Transition Economies." *Journal of Financial Intermediation* 23 (1):76–100. doi:10.1016/j.jfi.2013.11.003.

Poutsma, E. 2001. *Recent Trends in Employee Financial Participation in the European Union.* Dublin, Ireland: European Foundation for the Improvement of Living and Working Conditions.

Poutsma, E., J. R. Blasi, and D. L. Kruse. 2012. "Employee Share Ownership and Profit Sharing in Different Institutional Contexts." *The International Journal of Human Resource Management* 23 (8):1513–8. doi:10.1080/ 09585192.2012.661994.

Poutsma, E., and W. De Nijs. 2003. "Broad-Based Employee Financial Participation in the European Union." *The International Journal of Human Resource Management* 14 (6):863–92. doi:10.1080/0958519032000106128.

Poutsma, E., J. Hendrickx, and F. Huijgen. 2003. "Employee Participation in Europe: In Search of the Participative Workplace." *Economic and Industrial Democracy* 24 (1):45–76. doi:10.1177/0143831X03024001599.

Poutsma, E., P. Kalmi, and A. D. Pendleton. 2006. "The Relationship between Financial Participation and Other Forms of Employee Participation: New Survey Evidence from Europe." *Economic and Industrial Democracy* 27 (4):637–67. doi:10.1177/0143831X06069006.

Raith, M. 2003. "Competition, Risk, and Managerial Incentives." *American Economic Review* 93 (4):1425–36. doi: 10.1257/000282803769206395.

Romo, O. M. 2005. "Political Exchange and Bargaining Reform in Italy and Spain." *European Journal of Industrial Relations* 11 (1):7–26. doi:10.1177/0959680105050397.

Schmidt, V. A. 2007. "Bringing the State back into the Varieties of Capitalism and Discourse back into the Explanation of Change." Center for European Studies Program for the Study of Germany and Europe, Working Paper Series, 07.3, Harvard University, USA.

Tirole, J. 2001. "Corporate Governance." *Econometrica* 69 (1):1–35. doi:10.1111/1468-0262.00177.

Uchida, K. 2006. "Determinants of Stock Option Use by Japanese Companies." *Review of Financial Economics* 15 (3):251–69. doi:10.1016/j.rfe.2005.08.001.

Whitley, R. 1999. *Divergent Capitalisms: The Social Structuring and Change of Business Systems.* Oxford, UK: Oxford University Press.

Contemporary Human Resource Management Practices in Russia: Flexibility under Uncertainty

Veronika Kabalina, Olga Zelenova and Kira Reshetnikova

Abstract: This article develops the concept of flexibility in Human Resource Management (HRM) practices which can increase a company's potential to respond to substantial variation in the business environment. It reveals the characteristics of flexible HRM practices in Russian companies in an uncertain external and internal environment. Cranet survey data gathered from October 2014 until March 2015 is used for measuring the environmental uncertainty and flexibility of staffing, training, and development, pay, employee relations, and communication. A comparison of the flexibility indices for the four HRM practices shows a higher level of flexibility in training and development practices. The research results confirm a direct positive relationship between the complexity of the environment and the flexibility of HRM practices.

INTRODUCTION

In recent decades, flexibility as a characteristic of the behavior of organizations in an uncertain external environment has become the subject of scientific research. In a number of publications, it has been shown that Human Resource Management (HRM) flexibility can contribute to the overall flexibility of the organization (Bhattacharya, Gibson, and Doty 2005; Ketkar and Sett 2009; Martinez-Sanchez et al. 2007; Chang et al. 2013). The motivation for this article is to verify whether, in situations of high uncertainty in the Russian economy, Russian companies have developed flexible HRM practices (FHRMP) that have contributed to their adaptation to external and internal organizational changes.

The term "HRM flexibility" was formed in the context of market economies and was tied to an organization's performance, assuming a relative abundance of resources. This article studies FHRMP in a different context, under the conditions of rapid and drastic changes in the economic, political, and institutional environment, and scarce resources, both in terms of availability of investment and a skilled labor force. This context is typical for countries with transition economies. In the turbulent environment of a transition economy, companies try to persevere by retaining the core of the workforce[1]. The latter is particularly significant for Russia, considering the specific pattern of the locations of large manufacturing companies within small local communities ("company towns"). Notably, the Russian government's anti-crisis bailout plan, adopted in January 2015 in response to the deterioration of the economic situation in 2014–2015, was titled "Priority Measures for Supporting Stable Growth and Social Stability in 2015."

This article reveals the characteristics of the flexibility of HRM practices of Russian companies in an uncertain external and internal environment. To achieve this, the authors set the following four tasks: (1) justifying the notion of "the flexibility of HRM practices"; (2) measuring the degree of flexibility of HRM practices based on the data of the Russian part of the international study Cranet 2014; (3) characterizing the dynamism and complexity of the external and internal environment of companies; and (4) identifying the links between the flexibility of HRM practices and the characteristics of the organizational environment.

Overall, we make three contributions to the literature. First, we develop and validate the measurements of FHRMP in Russia. Secondly, we provide empirical evidence of the links between specific FHRMP and the characteristics of the organizational environment. Thirdly, we present an explanation of how FHRMP can contribute to a company's responsiveness to changing environments. Together, our findings demonstrate the strategic value of FHRMP and have practical implications for managers.

This article contains five sections. Section 2 includes an analysis of the main approaches to research into flexibility of HRM in general and in Russia in particular. Section 3 describes the major data source, measurements of the flexibility of HRM practice, and the dynamism and uncertainty of the external and internal organizational environments. Section 4 presents research results. Section 5 discusses the main findings, as well as caveats and constraints related to the study.

THEORETICAL BACKGROUND AND RESEARCH

HR Flexibility and HRM Practice Flexibility

Considering the flexibility of HRM practices in Russian organizations, we rely on the contextual perspective of strategic HRM theory and institutional theory. Current strategic HRM theory suggests that HR flexibility is an internal trait or characteristic of the firm, facilitating a firm's rapid response to a changing economic environment.

Institutional theory allows us to connect organizational and national perspectives and take into account a wider set of factors determining the behavior of organizations and explaining their flexibility patterns. A fundamental principle of the neo-institutional theory is that organizations are shaped according to the environment in which they are active (DiMaggio and Powell 1991; Meyer and Rowan 1991; Zucker 1991). They adopt practices that are socially legitimate—those that correspond to the regulatory, normative, and cognitive institutions in their respective environments. Hence, organizations that face the same set of environmental conditions tend to use similar practices (DiMaggio and Powell 1983).

While developing the concepts of fit and flexibility in the framework of strategic HRM, Wright and Snell (1998) stated that to maintain vertical alignment in uncertain competitive environments, firms need flexibly oriented HRM systems. They assert that any strategy should fit with three generic conceptual variables: HRM practices, employee skills, and employee behaviors. They defined flexibility as the extent to which a firm's human resources (HR) possess the skills and behavioral repertoires which can give a firm options for pursuing strategic alternatives in the firm's competitive environment, as well as the extent to which the necessary HRM practices can be quickly identified, developed, and implemented to maximize the flexibilities inherent in those HR. They further distinguished between the resource flexibility of HRM practices (the extent to which they can be adapted and applied across a variety of situations) and the coordination flexibility of HRM practices (how quickly the practices can be resynthesized, reconfigured, and redeployed). Although Wright and Snell posit the idea of flexible HRM systems, their study focuses on the flexibility of HR.

Subsequent work in this area also focused on flexibility of HR rather than FHRMP per se (Bhattacharya, Gibson, and Doty, 2005; Beltrán-Martín et al. 2008; Wu 2011; Chang et al. 2013). Chang et al. define flexible HRM systems as "a set of internally consistent HRM practices that enable a firm to acquire and develop HR for a wide range of alternative uses and to redeploy those resources quickly and effectively" (Chang et al. 2013, 1926). The application of flexibility to an organization's HR restricts FHRMP to those which shape the flexibility of HR, such as selectivity in recruitment, extensive training, formal performance appraisal, and pay for performance (Bhattacharya, Gibson, and Doty 2005; Way et al. 2015). However, these studies do not specifically address whether these practices are flexible. At the same time, the researchers assert that for the firm that has developed employee skills and behavior, this flexibility may help the company adapt to crises with its existing human resource base and avoid layoffs and turnover (Bhattacharya, Gibson, and Doty 2005). Thus, HRM flexibility can be considered from the point of view of adaptation to crisis conditions.

Flexibility in HRM is also interpreted in a narrow sense and often pertains to workplace and working hours flexibility considered in such forms of flexibility as numerical flexibility, functional flexibility, and temporal flexibility (Mayne, Tregaski, and Brewster 1996; Tregaskis et al. 1998; Richbell et al. 2011).

Some studies have investigated the effects of HRM flexibility on an organization's performance. The basis for this study is the hypothesis that HRM flexibility promotes innovation within organizations and enables faster responses to changes in the economic environment. The results of Bhattacharya, Gibson, and Doty (2005) showed that the components of HR flexibility—particularly HR practice flexibility—were highly correlated with high performance work practices and a significant independent effect on firm performance. Both a positive influence (Chang et al. 2013; Ketkar and Sett 2009; Martinez-Sanchez et al. 2007) and negative effects (Way et al. 2015) of FHRMP on an organization's performance have been identified.

Two Dimensions of FHRMP

Variety of methods

Drawing on the notion of "requisite variety," Weick (1979) and Bhattacharya, Gibson, and Doty (2005) state that a variety of HR practice with a more complex and varied set of routines provides firms with a greater ability to respond dynamically to changing and complex environments.

We expand the construct of HR practices which maximize the flexibility of HR to all key HRM practices which enhance a company's potential to respond to more substantial variation in the business environment. We assume that the organization should already have a set of HRM practices from which it can choose certain tools (e.g., methods, technologies, or routines), rather than create a new tool each time for a new situation. The variety of methods used in HRM practices is an important characteristic of their flexibility.

Autonomy in decision-making

The second feature of the flexibility of HRM practices is autonomy in making decisions on HRM policy-related issues. Autonomy is considered to be a characteristic that supports variability: it is the right of decision-makers to choose certain methods in managing people in an organization. The application of this right in practice leads to heterogeneity in HRM approaches and to a wider variety of methods.

The devolvement of HRM responsibilities to line managers and the outsourcing of HR activities to external providers have been considered primarily in terms of cost reduction or the impact on the strategic position of HR departments (Gooderham et al. 2015; Larsen and Brewster 2003; Reichel and Lazarova 2013). Using international Cranet data, Reichel and Lazarova (2013) show that outsourcing and the devolution of HRM functions to line managers could increase the flexibility, responsiveness, and innovation of HR departments. Their results suggest that the strategic position of HR departments is negatively influenced by devolution to line management and positively influenced by outsourcing noncore HR tasks. No significant effect of outsourcing core HR activities was found.

The interpretation of what exactly (tasks, responsibilities, decision-making power) is shared between line managers and HR specialists remains blurred in the literature. Discussing the limitation of the CRANET research, Larsen and Brewster (2003) draw attention to the fact that the term "major policy decisions" in the survey was determined by the respondents. It follows that it is impossible to clearly define what these decisions are (e.g., operational or strategic). In addition, the dividing line between policy and practice is not obvious on the ground (Larsen and Brewster 2003, 232).

Based on the CRANET data, Gooderham et al. (2015) examine the devolution of decision-making power, defined as the responsibility for making decisions on HRM issues related to staffing, training and development, pay, and industrial relations. They explain the focus on the decision-making power by its centrality to HRM, as opposed to HR tasks and responsibilities, which often represent the implementation of policy decisions made at a higher (or more central) level.

We believe that the devolution of decision-making to line managers in the relevant areas of HRM increases the variability and flexibility of HRM practices.

Research also shows that line manager involvement in HR is country specific (Brewster et al. 2006; Gooderham et al. 2015). In general, comparative studies in the field of HRM suggest that the country can be a key explanatory variable of HR policies and practices. Considering FHRMP in Russian companies, we need to take into account the national context factors, including institutional ones, as antecedents of the flexibility of HRM practices in Russia.

Research into flexibility of the Russian labor market

Since the beginning of the 1990s, Russian researchers have been studying flexibility from the standpoint of labor economics, sociology, management, and HRM. Flexibility was identified (Kapelyushnikov 2001) as one of the key characteristics of the Russian labor market in the transformation period, starting with the launch of market reforms in 1992. A comparative analysis of labor markets in Russia and in Central and Eastern Europe made it possible to talk about a special "Russian model" of the transformational processes in the sphere of employment. This model is characterized by such features as extreme flexibility, mobility, and high adaptability. Kapeliushnikov notes that the Russian labor market is less "regulated" than the labor markets of other post-socialist countries, and labor market flexibility takes on special significance during the transition stages of economic development. Labor market flexibility as a special adaptive mechanism was seen less in reducing the number of employees, but more in wage flexibility, and in the duration and intensity of the decrease in real wages, systematic delays in payment, hidden wages, and forced part-time employment. The special path that the Russian labor market was taking was noticed by Western researchers (e.g., Layard and Richter 1995).

Subsequent research relates to the verification of the viability and evaluation of the prospects for the development of the Russian labor market flexibility model and its application. Its social and economic consequences were assessed more critically. It was recognized that labor market flexibility allowed the startup costs of the transition to new business conditions to be paid off, while it became an obstacle to the effective restructuring of employment in Russia. There was a huge gap between the normative and actual characteristics of the labor market. If the legal framework of the Russian labor market was rigid and overregulated, the real mechanisms of its functioning were characterized by a high degree of flexibility and mobility. This gap was due to the dominance of informal institutions, norms and practices, and the ineffectiveness of the Russian system of law enforcement (e.g., Kapelyushnikov 2003; Gimpelson and Kapeliushnikov 2013).

The study of various forms of work and wage formation in Russia reflected this gap (e.g., Gimpel'son, Kapelyushnikov, and Ratnikova 2003; Gimpel'son and Kapeliushnikov 2006; Kapeliushnikov et al. 2006; Gimpelson and Kapeliushnikov 2008; Kapeliushnikov, Kuznetsov and Kuznetsova 2012). The spread of informal labor relations is an effective way to increase the flexibility and adaptation of the labor market to a recession economy, but in a growing economy this advantage turns into a systemic brake for increasing labor productivity. The sustainability of such a model in the future is also under question.

The degree of real wage flexibility in connection with the level of unemployment in Russia has been evaluated in a number of studies. Significant negative relationships between wages and unemployment with elasticity close to −0.1 were found in all cases (Shilov and Meller 2008), as were found between unemployment and various inflation indicators (Gafarov 2011). Referring to these results, the researchers assert that the mechanism introduced in Russia in the early 2000s can be described by a Phillips curve. Later, testing three basic Phillips curve models, Vakulenko and Gurvich (2016) reveal high real wage flexibility and concluded that the Russian labor market was able to return quickly to the full utilization of labor resources. This ability was confirmed in the crises of 2008–2009 and 2015–2016. The flexibility of real wages was viewed as a sign of an effective labor market, where the operation of market mechanisms is not limited to excessive regulation. The findings are partly consistent with the hypothesis discussed above on the specifics of the Russian labor market model (adaptation to shocks primarily through wages and not unemployment).

Russian labor market flexibility meant the market continued to be reasonably stable to subsequent crisis changes in the external environment. Despite the growing economic difficulties from the end of 2012, when the Russian economy entered a period of slowing economic growth and stagnation, key labor market indicators continued to remain at favorable levels, although they began to react to the deterioration of the economic situation with a delay. This stability is based on a certain institutional configuration that distinguishes the Russian labor market (Gimpel'son and Kapelyushnikov 2015). However, it is noted that short-term fluctuations are subject to a number of long-term structural factors that will seriously affect the functioning of the Russian labor market in the medium and long term (Kapelyushnikov and Oshchepkov 2014).

Summing up the research on labor market flexibility, labor economists proceed from the understanding of flexibility precisely as the adaptability of the labor market to real constant and unique shocks (crises and reforms), studying the situation at the macro level, while processes that occur within real organizations remain behind the scenes.

Studies on HRM practices and flexibility at the micro level

In order to answer the question on how Russian companies adapt employment and HRM policies and practices to changes in the external environment, studies on HRM practices and flexibility at the micro level have been conducted by sociologists and researchers in management and HRM since the early 1990s; however, these studies are not yet numerous.

One of the first research projects in this field was implemented by the Russian Institute for Comparative Labor Relations Research (ISITO) in cooperation with the Center for Comparative Labor Studies University of Warwick with the support of Economic and Social Research Council (ESRC) in 1992–1994 and 2004–2005 (e.g. Clarke 2007; Clarke 1999; Kabalina 1997, 1998, 2005) The cross-cutting theme of the study was the process of restructuring and transforming a traditional Soviet enterprise into a capitalist one, which was based on a change in its objective function and changes in the management structure (above all, HRM). It was found that one of the targets of Russian enterprises in the transition period of the 1990s was survival, the condition of which was the preservation of labor collectives. Not making decisions about staff reduction was a rational strategy in the face of uncertain economic conditions and the weakness of social support institutions. Companies could not ignore the demands that came from the state, primarily from regional authorities, for the preservation of social stability in local communities, which is understood, first of all, to mean preserving jobs and curbing unemployment. ISITO studies also showed that the uncertainties of production and supply in the HRM system had to be administered flexibly, and punishments and rewards were discretionary. Line managers (shop chiefs and foremen) had a high degree of authority, although the much tighter control of spending meant that their discretion was significantly reduced (Clarke 1999; Kabalina 1998).

ISITO research tested the hypothesis that new business organizations without a Soviet past created using private funds would be less burdened by traditional Soviet management practices, and therefore, their adaptation to new market conditions will be different and more modern than traditional ones. However, it was found that the new organizations had to be reinvented in the system of state protection, without having established connections. As a result, both new and older organizations often demonstrated similar market practices. The development HRM proceeded according to residual principles. Strong evidence for greater management effectiveness in the organizations of the new private sector was not found (Kabalina 2005).

Nevertheless, it was found that changes in HRM, as a rule, occurred with changing external conditions. Practices changed only when the enterprise became better established and began to focus on the market. New HRM practices supported efforts to increase the efficiency of production and strengthen the viability of the organization.

The attributes of Soviet HRM practices continued to be reproduced in Russian organizations, such as the low status and decentralization of HRM. For corporate management practices and culture, organizations revived Soviet traditions in combination with elements of Western thinking style. This was due to the need to master international business standards and culture (Kabalina 2005).

The results of the Cranet International Research Network on Human Resource Management project, implemented in Russia in 2008–2009, revealed further changes in HRM practices in Russia (e.g., Gurkov et al. 2009; Gurkov, Zelenova, and Saidov 2012; Gurkov et al. 2014). They confirmed that Russian organizations not only preserved the Soviet tradition of flexible working hours (overtime, work on weekends, part-time work, extended shifts), but also added new flexible forms of employment (short-term employment contracts and casual employment). The researchers identified two features of personnel management—highly flexible working hours and the low formalization of staff assessment. The wider rights of line managers for recruitment, payment, and staffing, combined with the minimal formalization of employee assessment, gave management almost unlimited opportunities for staff reductions.

The 1992–1998 experience was not in vain for Russian companies; the Russian HRM system in relatively prosperous times had been "sharpened" for the crisis. The existing system offered additional opportunities to save costs and increase labor intensity by using flexible working hours. In addition, organizations have significant reserves of flexibility in contractual relationships—the expansion of fixed-term labor contracts and casual employment (Gurkov et al. 2009).

An analysis of modern HRM practices confirms that Russian organizations actively use fixed-term contracts to reduce labor costs and adapt to changes in demand, and to increase productivity and the flexibility of labor relations. However, fixed-term contracts can reduce the likelihood of innovation, as they reduce investment in human capital, which leads to a decline in labor productivity. The results show that fixed-term contracts have a positive impact on innovation only when they are used sparingly. With the increase in the share of workers with fixed contract terms, the probability of innovative activity of enterprises decreases (Smirnykh 2016).

The study of the flexibility of HRM practices in Russia is characteristic not only of large-scale research projects, but also of research at branch level (Zelenova and Prosvirkina 2016) and even at the level of individual projects within the organization (Romanenko and Apen'ko 2016). These studies support the general trends identified.

DATA AND MEASURES

The empirical basis for studying the flexibility of HRM practices was the result of the Cranet 2014 survey. Data were collected between October 2014 and March 2015; 131 questionnaires were collected, covering the almost 1.8 million employees in the companies surveyed. In the questionnaire, the heads of the HR departments of small, medium, and large companies participated (see Table 1). The structure of the sample by field of activity indicates that the companies represent mainly the industrial sectors of the economy (see Figure 1). The study used a purposive sample that does not claim to be generalized across all Russian companies. It characterizes large companies (2/3 of the sample) working primarily in the industrial sector of the Russian economy located in the main economic regions of the country. In general, we can assume that the results of the study characterize the flexibility of HRM practices in the main segments of the Russian economy.

Measures

FHRMP metrics

A variety of methods was chosen to characterize FHRMP. This characteristic is considered separately in relation to the four groups of FHRMP (staffing, training, and development, pay,

TABLE 1
Sample Structure by Company Size

Companies by size	Number of staff, people	Number of companies	Share
Small firms	100–250	26	20%
Medium companies	251–500	16	12%
Large companies	501–1000	32	24%
	1,001–5,000	34	26%
Extra-large companies	More than 5,000	23	18%
Total		131	100%

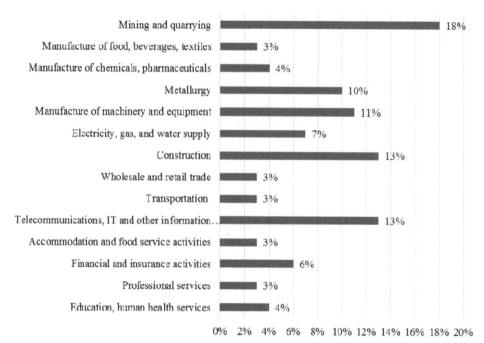

FIGURE 1. Sample structure by industries

employee relations, and communication). Each practice includes a set of methods, which are described by empirical indicators based on the Cranet 2014 questionnaire variables (see Table 2).

For example, the FHRMP of staffing included ways to reduce staff and costs, attracting and selecting staff, using flexible forms of employment and working hours, and special recruiting programs for different categories of employees. The methods to reduce the staff and costs were recruitment freezes, early retirement, internal transfer, redundancy, voluntary redundancies, no renewal of fixed term contracts, vacations, outsourcing, management pay-cuts, overtime bans, wage freezes, reduced job proportions, job sharing, reduced benefits, employee pay-cuts, individual layoffs, concentrated layoffs, and mass layoffs/compulsory redundancies.

The second characteristic of FHRM practices is where the decision-making power lies. This includes two metrics with subsequent empirical indicators: first, the distribution of responsibility in solving HRM issues between line managers and HR service, and second, outsourcing HR functions.

Environmental metrics

Uncertainty of the environment was characterized by the dynamism and complexity of the external and internal environment of the organization, presented in Table 3.

TABLE 2
Variety of HRM Practices: CRANET 2014 Empirical Indicators

HRM practices	Empirical indicators
Staffing	Methods to downsize the organization and reduce the costs
	Recruitment methods
	Selection methods
	Flexible employment methods
	Recruitment programs for specific groups of people
Training and development	Career management methods
	Training and career progression programs for specific groups of people
Pay	Compensation forms
	Benefit schemes
Employee relations and communication	Methods used for employees to communicate their views to management

TABLE 3
Characteristics of Organizational Environment: CRANET 2014 Empirical Indicators

Characteristics	Empirical indicators
Dynamism of the external environment	Changes in the market(s) an organization currently serves
Dynamism of the internal environment	Organizational changes in the last 3 years
Complexity of the external environment	Main market(s) for the organization's products or services
Complexity of the internal environment	Estimates of gross revenue over the past 3 years
	Estimates of trade union influence

The characteristics, metrics, and empirical indicators form a three-level system for measuring the flexibility of HR practices and environmental uncertainty. They were used to calculate as follows: (1) the index of the flexibility of each practice, taking into account the two characteristics (variety of methods and decision-making power); (2) the overall flexibility index for all HRM practices (FHRMI) based on partial indices—the variety of methods index (VMI) and decision-making power index (DMPI); (3) indices of dynamism and complexity and the organizational environment; and (5) correlating the complexity and dynamic indices of the organizational environment with FHRMI.

When calculating the indices, intermediate indicators were reduced to a uniform dimension, taking into account the normality of the distribution of the indicators: minimum flexibility, medium flexibility, or maximum flexibility. Summing the resulting one-dimensional variables, we calculated the corresponding indices.

RESULTS

FHRMI

For all four HRM practices (staffing, training and development, pay, employee relations), calculations were made and indices formed, which are given in Table 4 in the form of the distribution of the companies into three levels of flexibility (minimum, medium, maximum). Below, the results obtained are discussed with allowance for intermediate calculations.

TABLE 4
Organizational distribution according to levels of flexibility in HRM practices (1-minimum, 2-medium, 3-maximum)

HRM practices	Frequency	%	%
Staffing			
1	14	10.7	20.0
2	41	31.3	58.6
3	15	11.5	21.4
Valid	70	53.4	100.0
Missing	61	46.6	
N	131	100.0	
Training and development			
1	12	9.2	13.2
2	49	37.4	53.8
3	30	22.9	33.0
Valid	91	69.5	100.0
Missing	40	30.5	
N	131	100.0	
Pay			
1	15	11.5	15.5
2	60	45.8	61.9
3	22	16.8	22.7
Valid	97	74.0	100.0
Missing	34	26.0	
N	131	100.0	
Employee relations and communication			
1	11	8.4	11.6
2	63	48.1	66.3
3	21	16.0	22.1
Valid	95	72.5	100.0
Missing	36	27.5	
N	131	100.0	
Variety of methods index (VMI)			
1	12	9.2	23.1
2	30	22.9	57.7
3	10	7.6	19.2
Valid	52	39.7	100.0
Missing	79	60.3	
N	131	100.0	
Decision-making power index (DMPI)			
1	21	16.0	22.1
2	56	42.7	58.9
3	18	13.7	18.9
Valid	95	72.5	100.0
Missing	36	27.5	
N	131	100.0	
Overall flexibility index for all HRM practices (FHRMI)			
1	10	7.6	22.2
2	25	19.1	55.6
3	10	7.6	22.2
Valid	45	34.4	100.0
Missing	86	65.6	
N	131	100.0	

In general, staffing practices in Russian companies have minimum and medium flexibility. In terms of reducing staff and costs; for example, 48 percent of companies demonstrate minimum flexibility in terms of the variety of practices used and only 10 percent show maximum flexibility. Minimum flexibility (62 percent) is shown in terms of the availability of special recruiting programs for different categories of personnel. The remaining characteristics of the flexibility index for staffing practices are at the medium level or slightly above.

The flexibility of training and development practices is generally higher than staffing practices due to the wide variety of career management methods: the medium level of flexibility is observed in 37 percent of companies, and the maximum level in 26 percent. However, special programs for training and development of different categories of employees are practically unused, which leads to a decrease in the level of flexibility of training and development practices. In terms of 'decision-making power', companies have the medium level of flexibility with respect to training and development practices.

In pay practices, almost a third of companies (29%) demonstrate the maximum level of flexibility in using different compensation forms. Flexibility in terms of the diversity of social benefits is lower: 34 percent of cases are at the medium level and 28 percent at the maximum level.

The second indicator of "decision-making power" demonstrates multidirectional trends. Most companies (54%) have the medium level of flexibility with regard to who makes decisions on pay. There is less flexibility in outsourcing practices: 61 percent of companies demonstrate the minimum level. In general, in 62 percent of the companies the flexibility of personnel pay practices is at the medium level.

The flexibility of employee relations and communication in regards to the variety of methods used is at the medium level in 44 percent of companies. In terms of "decision-making power," flexibility is minimum for who is responsible for making decisions in this area (in 44% of companies there is the minimum level of flexibility) and for outsourcing (83% of companies have minimum flexibility). A comparison of the flexibility indices for the four HRM practices shows that, in general, there is a higher level of flexibility in the training and development of staff.

The FHRMI was calculated on the basis of two indices VMI and DMPI (see Table 4). When calculating the partial indices, there was a significant increase in the number of missed answers about the implementation of all practices and the distribution of responsibilities and outsourcing. In the index of flexibility in the degree of differentiation of HRM practices, information from 79 respondents out of 131 was missing; in the flexibility index for the implementation of HRM practices information from 36 was missing. In the general index of flexibility of HRM practices, the number of missed answers was 86.

As a result, the overall flexibility of HRM practices in Russian companies can be characterized as at the medium level (see Table 4). A summary for all FHRMI, indicating the average values (mean), is presented in Table 5.

Uncertainty Indices of the Organizational Environment

The uncertainty of the organizational environment was determined by four characteristics: the dynamism and the complexity of the external and the internal environments. The

TABLE 5
FHRMP Indices

Indices	Mean
Flexibility index of staffing practices	2.01
Flexibility index of training and development practices	2.20
Flexibility index of pay practices	2.07
Flexibility index of employee relations and communication	2.11
Variety of methods index	1.96
Decision-making power index	1.97
Overall flexibility index for all HRM practices	2.00

dynamism of the external environment was measured by current changes in the market in which the company operates. Forty-one percent of companies characterize the market as stable. A third (32%) note slight negative dynamics, 14 percent said the market fell significantly, and 13 percent said the market grew.

To assess the dynamism of the internal environment of the organization, an indicator of the organization's boundaries over the last 3 years was used. For 16 percent of companies, the changes were related to the acquisition of another company and 10 percent of the companies' mergers. In general, the internal dynamism of the environment is low, since in most cases there were no changes in the company boundaries. The calculation of the dynamic environment index shows that the internal and external organizational environments in most cases is perceived by companies as weakly dynamic (58%), for 32 percent the environment is stable, and only 10 percent of cases indicate a strongly dynamic environment.

The complexity of the external environment is related to the scale of the market in which the organization operates (local, regional, national, continent-wide, world-wide). The higher the market level, the more complex the organizational environment, since in this case the number of factors the company should respond to increases as does the level of variability of each of these factors. Only 2 percent of companies are oriented towards local markets, which is not surprising, since the survey conditions did not involve the participation of small firms, and 18 percent towards regional markets. Forty-one percent of companies work in the Russian market and the same number of companies in foreign markets, which indicates a greater complexity of the external environment for a significant number of companies.

A serious problem was the assessment of the complexity of the internal environment for the limited number of indicators that were presented in the questionnaire. It was evaluated through indicators of revenue for the last three years and the influence of trade unions in the organization.

We assumed that the revenue indicator characterizes the ability of management to respond to challenges faced by the company: the lower the revenue, the more complex the internal environment of the company becomes. More than half of the companies received revenues in the last three years, either significantly exceeding costs (16%) or sufficient to generate small profits (50%). About one-third of companies (28%) managed to cover costs, and only 6 percent of companies estimated the revenue received as insufficient to cover costs.

The influence of trade unions in the organization was considered to be an important indicator of the influence of staff on the complexity of the internal environment, as with its growth, the number of factors within the company that the organization is forced to react to is increasing. In almost 40 percent of cases, trade unions do not exert any influence on the activities of the organization. The perceived maximum degree of influence, which increases the complexity of the internal environment, was found in 35 percent of companies. For 45 percent of Russian organizations, the complexity of the organizational environment was average, and considered low by 32 percent of them. In general, it can be assumed that Russian companies feel sufficiently adapted to their organizational environment.

The Relationship between the FHRMP and the Organizational Environment

To determine the relationship between FHRMP and the dynamism and complexity of the organizational environment, a correlation analysis was performed using Pearson's coefficient (see Table 6).

The results of this analysis show that there is a weak negative correlation between the dynamism index and the flexibility index of training and development practices (Pearson's correlation coefficient is -0.27). This means that the higher the dynamism of the organizational environment, the lower the flexibility of practices in training and developing staff. It can be assumed that this is not quite the usual effect as in a changing market situation and with other organizational changes, the problems of using a variety of training methods, their differentiation, and the choice of who is responsible for the implementation recede into the background. Companies are trying to maintain a certain "status quo" in matters of employee training.

The flexibility index of staff pay practices is positively and fairly closely related to the index of complexity of the organizational environment (Pearson coefficient 0.45). In a more complex organizational environment, the flexibility of pay practices will be higher. A similar picture is observed according to the index of flexibility in the variety of HRM practices (Pearson coefficient 0.47). We can say that in a complex organizational environment, companies are forced to diversify their HRM practices. This fact seemed to influence the positive and close correlation between the general FHRMPI and the complexity index of the organizational environment (Pearson coefficient 0.35).

The dynamic index of the organizational environment is practically unrelated to the indices of flexibility of HRM practices (except for the flexibility index of training and development practices described above). This result could be influenced by the fact that the dynamic index was calculated using the dynamics for different periods (in one case for three years, in the other for the current moment).

CONCLUSIONS

This article developed the construct of flexibility in HRM practices which embraces staffing, training and development, pay, and labor relations, and which can increase a company's

TABLE 6

Correlations between FHRMPI and Indices of the Uncertainty of the Organizational Environment

	Dynamic environment index	Complexity index of the organizational environment
Flexibility index of staffing practices		
Pearson coefficient	0.09	−0.07
Level (two-tailed)	0.88	0.59
N	68	56
Flexibility index of training and development practices		
Pearson coefficient	−0.27*	0.14
Level (two-tailed)	0.01	0.26
N	85	64
Flexibility index of pay practices		
Pearson coefficient	−0.02	0.45**
Level (two-tailed)	0.85	0.00
N	89	68
Flexibility index of employee relations and communication		
Pearson coefficient	−0.02	0.18
Level (two-tailed)	0.86	0.14
N	91	72
Variety of methods index		
Pearson coefficient	−0.12	0.47**
Level (two-tailed)	0.41	0.00
N	51	40
Decision-making power index		
Pearson coefficient	0.04	−0.19
Level (two-tailed)	0.68	0.11
N	89	72
Overall flexibility index for all HRM practices		
Pearson coefficient	−.10	.35*
Level (two-tailed)	.51	.03
N	44	37

  **Correlation is significant at a 0.01 level (two-tailed).
  *Correlation is significant at a 0.05 level (two-tailed).

potential to respond to substantial variation in the business environment. A comparison of the flexibility indices for the four HRM practices showed a higher level of flexibility in training and development practices. This finding confirms the proposition that HRM flexibility practice maximizes the flexibilities inherent in those HR.

When analyzing the results of the study, we developed a number of indices that characterize the flexibility of HRM practices. If data are collected using the same toolkit in different countries or at different time periods, this allows comparative studies and an analysis of the results in different (or similar) organizational environments (Lazarova, Morley, and Tyson 2008). In addition, the use of these indices in the analysis of the external and internal organizational environment will allow further, deeper analysis (factorial, cluster analysis) to identify the main trends, and possibly patterns, associated with the development of HRM practices under different environmental conditions of the organization.

The study revealed a direct positive relationship between the complexity of the environment and the flexibility of HRM practices. The values of the flexibility index using a variety of methods, and the overall flexibility index for all HRM practices are higher if companies have more complex revenue conditions and higher when the overall complexity of the environment is estimated. In other words, more flexible practices are formed in more complex environments.

Since in our study the complexity of the environment grows with the growth of the market, it can be assumed that for those Russian companies that work in international markets, there is a lot of flexibility in HRM practices. In other words, the international environment favorably affects the range of tools available and the flexibility of HRM practices. This conclusion is partially confirmed by the results of the analysis of data in the context of industries. Higher values of FHRMPI were found in the companies of those industries whose products are sold on world markets. These results can be considered preliminary due to a small number of observations in industries with international business orientation. Nevertheless, they suggest that a new model of flexibility is being formed in a number of industries in the Russian economy, the elements of which are already formed under the influence not only of Russian realities, but also of global competition.

Attention also needs to be paid to the weak feedback of the dynamism index with the index of flexibility of staff training and development. Such a non-trivial result raises the issue of forming a more complex, dynamic model of the flexibility of HRM practices, taking into account the multidirectional impact of the complexity and dynamism of the environment. In particular, we assume that a complex environment promotes the development of HRM practices, the formation of a variety of methods which companies rely on when adapting to a dynamic environment. Tackling this issue and the hypothesis presupposes longitudinal studies.

The correlation analysis shows there is no connection between the indices of flexibility of HRM practices and the indices of the dynamic nature of the environment. An explanation for this could be found in organizational inertia. This term was proposed in the 1960s. Stinchcombe (1965), who understood this to be the tendency of an organization to maintain the basic features and ways of functioning that emanated from its inception. It is characteristic that these features are a reflection of the social, cultural, and technical conditions of the time of an organization's formation, rather than its subsequent adaptation to a changing environment. Many of the large Russian companies included in the survey sample have been developing since the Soviet era (although it is not always possible to ascertain that from the survey as many were only formally created as joint-stock companies after the 1990s). HRM practices as social institutions are rooted precisely in social and cultural conditions and are directly related to the actual (and not formal) time of organization. Therefore, we can assume that some inertia is associated with HRM practices, and it is in them that the desire of the organization to resist changes in the external and internal organizational environment is manifested.

However, it is quite possible that the reason for the weak connection between the indices of flexibility of HRM practices and dynamism is that there are a small number of indicators characterizing the external and internal environment of the organization, or their random selection, which we consider to be an objective constraint. CRANET is focused on the monitoring of HRM practices in companies operating in different market and institutional contexts and relies on proven tools (Lazarova, Morley, and Tyson 2008; Parry, Stavrou-Costea, and Morley 2011). The study of the organizational environment in its entirety is not its goal. A way to overcome this limitation may be to carry out further studies of the influence of the organizational environment on the flexibility characteristics of HRM practices, based on a specially developed toolkit.

Note

1. "The priority of Russian traditional enterprises through the 1990s was to survive the crisis, and in terms of personnel management this meant trying to hold on to the core of their labor force through the period of decline, in the hope of a subsequent recovery" (Clarke 2007, 127).

REFERENCES

Beltrán-Martín, I., V. Roca-Puig, A. Escrig-Tena, and J. C. Bou-Llusar. 2008. "Human Resource Flexibility as a Mediating Variable between High Performance Work Systems and Performance." *Journal of Management* 34 (5): 1009–44. doi:10.1177/0149206308318616.

Bhattacharya, M., D. Gibson, and D. H. Doty. 2005. "The Effects of Flexibility in Employee Skills, Employee Behaviors, and HR Practices on Firm Performance." *Journal of Management* 31 (4):622–40. doi:10.1177/0149206304272347.

Brewster, C., G. Wood, M. Brookes, and J. Van Ommeren. 2006. "What Determines the Size of the HR Function: A Cross-National Analysis." *Human Resource Management* 45 (1):3–21. doi:10.1002/hrm.20093.

Chang, S., Y. Gong, S. A. Way, and L. Jia. 2013. "Flexibility-Oriented HRM Systems, Absorptive Capacity, and Market Responsiveness and Firm Innovativeness." *Journal of Management* 39 (7):1924–51. doi:10.1177/0149206312466145.

Clarke, S. 1999. *The Formation of a Labor Market in Russia*. Cheltenham, UK: Edward Elgar.

Clarke, S. 2007. *The Development of Capitalism in Russia*. London, UK and New York, NY: Routledge.

DiMaggio, P. J., and W. W. Powell. 1983. "The Iron Cage Revisited: Institutional Isomorphism and Collective Rationality in Organizational Fields." *American Sociological Review* 48 (2):147–60. doi:10.2307/2095101.

DiMaggio, P. J., and W. W. Powell. 1991. "The Iron Cage Revisited: Institutional Isomorphism and Collective Rationality in Organizational Fields." In *The New Institutionalism in Organizational Analysis*, edited by W. W. Powell and P. J. DiMaggio, 195–200. Chicago, IL: University of Chicago Press.

Gimpelson, V., and R. Kapeliushnikov. 2013. "Labor Market Adjustment: Is Russia Different?" In *The Oxford Handbook of the Russian Economy*, edited by S. Weber and M. V. Alexeev. Oxford, UK: Oxford University Press.

Gooderham, P. N., M. J. Morley, E. Parry, and E. Stavrou. 2015. "National and Firm-Level Drivers of the Devolution of HRM Decision Making to Line Managers." *Journal of International Business Studies* 46 (6): 715–23. doi:10.1057/jibs.2015.5.

Gurkov, I., O. Zelenova, and Z. Saidov. 2012. "Mutation of HRM Practices in Russia: An Application of CRANET Methodology." *The International Journal of Human Resource Management* 23 (7):1289–302. doi:10.1080/09585192.2011.581633.

Gurkov, I., E. Morgunov, A. Settles, and O. Zelenova. 2014. "HRM in Russia over a Century of Storm and Turmoil: A Tale of Unrealized Dreams." In *The Development of Human Resource Management across Nations: Unity and Diversity*, edited by B. E. Kaufman. Cheltenham, UK – Northampton, Ma, USA: Edward Elgar.

Kapeliushnikov, R., V. Gimpelson, D. Brown, J. Earle, and H. Lehmann. 2006. "Nonstandard Forms and Measures of Employment and Unemployment in Transition: A Comparative Study of Estonia, Romania and Russia." *Comparative Economic Studies* 48 (3):435–57. doi:10.1057/palgrave.ces.8100181.

Kapeliushnikov, R., A. Kuznetsov, and O. Kuznetsova. 2012. "The Role of the Informal Sector, Flexible Working Time and Pay in the Russian Labor Market Model." *Post-Communist Economies* 24 (2):177–90. doi:10.1080/14631377.2012.675154.

Ketkar, S., and P. K. Sett. 2009. "HR Flexibility and Firm Performance: Analysis of a Multi-Level Causal Model." *The International Journal of Human Resource Management* 20 (5):1009–38. doi:10.1080/09585190902850240.

Larsen, H. H., and C. Brewster. 2003. "Line Management Responsibility for HRM: What Is Happening in Europe?" *Employee Relations* 25 (3):228–44. doi:10.1108/01425450310475838.

Layard, R., and A. Richter. 1995. "Labor Market Adjustment: The Russian Way." In *Russian Economic Reform at Risk*, edited by A. Aslund, 119–48. London, UK: Pinter.

Lazarova, M., M. Morley, and S. Tyson. 2008. "International Comparative Studies in HRM and Performance – the Cranet Data." *The International Journal of Human Resource Management* 19 (11):1995–2003. doi:10.1080/09585190802404239.

Martinez-Sanchez, A., M. Perez-Perez, P. De-Luis-Carnicer, and M. J. Vela-Jimenez. 2007. "Telework, Human Resources Flexibility and Firm Performance." *New Technology, Work and Employment* 22 (3):208–23. doi:10.1111/j.1468-005X.2007.00195.x.

Mayne, L., O. Tregaski, and C. Brewster. 1996. "A Comparative Analysis of the Link between Flexibility and HRM Strategy." *Employee Relations* 18 (3):5–24. doi:10.1108/01425459610116447.

Meyer, J. W., and B. Rowan. 1991. "Institutionalized Organizations: Formal Structure as Myth and Ceremony." In *The New Institutionalism in Organizational Analysis*, edited by W.W. Powell and P.J. DiMaggio. Chicago, IL: University of Chicago Press.

Parry, E., E. Stavrou-Costea, and M. J. Morley. 2011. "The Cranet International Research Network on Human Resource Management in Retrospect and Prospect." *Human Resource Management Review* 21 (1):1–4. doi:10.1016/j.hrmr.2010.09.006.

Reichel, A., and M. Lazarova. 2013. "The Effects of Outsourcing and Devolvement on the Strategic Position of the HR Function." *Human Resource Management* 52 (6):923–46. doi:10.1002/hrm.21577.

Richbell, S., M. Brookes, C. Brewster, and G. Wood. 2011. "Non-Standard Working Time: An International and Comparative Analysis." *The International Journal of Human Resource Management* 22 (4):945–62. doi:10.1080/09585192.2011.555135.

Smirnykh, L. I. 2016. "Is Flexible Labor Good for Innovation? Evidence from Russian Firm-Level Data." *Foresight and STI Governance* 4:60–70. doi:10.17323/1995-459X.2016.4.60.70..

Stinchcombe, A. L. 1965. "Social Structure and Organizations." In *Handbook of Organizations*, edited by J. G. March, 153–93. Chicago, IL: Rand McNally.

Tregaskis, O., C. Brewster, L. Mayne, and A. Hegewisch. 1998. "Flexible Working in Europe: The Evidence and the Implications." *European Journal of Work, Organization and Psychology* 7 (1):61–78.

Way, S. A., J. B. Tracey, C. H. Fay, P. M. Wright, S. A. Snell, S. Chang, and Y. Gong. 2015. "Validation of a Multidimensional HR Flexibility Measure." *Journal of Management* 41 (4):1098–131. doi:10.1177/0149206312463940.

Weick, K. E. 1979. *The Social Psychology of Organizing*. Reading, MA: Addison-Wesley.

Wright, P. M., and S. A. Snell. 1998. "Toward a Unifying Framework for Exploring Fit and Flexibility in Strategic Human Resource Management." *Academy of Management Review* 23 (4):756–72. doi:10.5465/amr.1998.1255637.

Wu, S.-H. 2011. "Impact of Environmental Uncertainty on Human Resource Flexibility." In *International Conference on Business and Economics Research*, 1277–81. Kuala Lumpur, IACSIT Press.

Zucker, L. G. 1991. "The Role of Institutionalization in Cultural Persistence." In *The New Institutionalism in Organizational Analysis*, edited by W. W. Powell and P. J. DiMaggio. Chicago, IL: University of Chicago Press.

REFERENCES IN RUSSIAN

Gafarov, B. N. 2011. "Krivaya Fillipsa i Stanovleniye Rynka Truda v Rossii." *Ekonomicheskiy zhurnal VSHE* 2: 155–76.

Gimpel'son, V. E., R. I. Kapelyushnikov, and T. A. Ratnikova. 2003. "Veliki li Glaza u Strakha? Strakh Bezrabotitsy i Gibkost' Zarabotnoy Platy v Rossii." *Problemy Rynka Truda, WP3. Vysshaya Shkola Ekonomiki*, 4.

Gimpel'son, V. E., and R. I. Kapelyushnikov (eds). 2006. Nestandartnaya Zanyatost' v Rossiyskoy Ekonomike. Moscow: Izdatel'skiy dom GU-VSHE.

Gimpel'son, V. E., and R. I. Kapelyushnikov (eds). 2008. Zarabotnaya Plata v Rossii: Evolyutsiya i Differentsiatsiya. Moscow: Izdatel'skiy dom GU VSHE.

Gimpel'son, V. E., and R. I. Kapelyushnikov. 2015. "Rossiyskaya Model' Rynka Truda: Ispytaniye Krizisom." *Zhurnal Novoy Ekonomicheskoy Assotsiatsii* 2:249–54.

Gurkov, I. B., O. I. Zelenova, A. S. Gol'dberg, and Z. B. Saidov. 2009. "Sistema Upravleniya Personalom na Rossiyskikh Firmakh v Zerkale Mezhdunarodnogo Sravneniya." *Mir Rossii* 3:132–50.

Kabalina, V.I. (ed). 1997. *Enterprise and Market: Dynamics of Management and Labour Relations in a Transition Period*. Moscow, Russia: ROSSPEN.

Kabalina, V. I. 1998. "Changes in Functions and Status of Line Managers." *Sociological Research* 5:34–43.

Kabalina, V.I. (ed). 2005. *Personnel Management Practices in the Contemporary Russian Enterprises*. Moscow: ISITO.

Kapelyushnikov, R. I. 2001. *Rossiyskiy Rynok Truda: Adaptatsiya Bez Restrukturizatsii. M.*: Moscow: Izdatel'skiy Dom GU-VSHE.

Kapelyushnikov, R. I. 2003. "Rossiyskaya Model' Rynka Truda: Chto Vperedi?" *Voprosy Ekonomiki* 4:83–100.

Kapelyushnikov, R. I., and A. Yu. Oshchepkov. 2014. "Rossiyskiy Rynok Truda: Paradoksy Postkrizisnogo Razvitiya." *Problemy Rynka Truda. WP3. Vysshaya Shkola Ekonomiki*, 4.

Romanenko, M. A., and S. N. Apen'ko. 2016. "Vliyaniye Gibkikh Tekhnologiy na Upravleniye Chelovecheskimi Resursami Proyektov Predpriyatiy." *Fundamental'nyye Issledovaniya* 9 (2):411–8. [Elektronnyy resurs] https://fundamental-research.ru/ru/article/view?id=40759 (data obrashcheniya: 23.05.2017).

Shilov, A., and Y. Meller. 2008. "Krivaya Zarabotnykh Plat: Teoriya i Empirika." *Kvantil* 4:93–100.

Vakulenko, E. S., and E. T. Gurvich. 2016. "Gibkost' Real'noy Zarabotnoy Platy v Rossii: Sravnitel'nyy Analiz." *Zhurnal Novoy Ekonomicheskoy Assotsiatsii* 3 (31):67–92.

Zelenova, O. I., and E. Yu. Prosvirkina. 2016. "Vliyaniye Vneshney Sredy na Praktiki Upravleniya Chelovecheskimi Resursami v Rossiyskom Bankovskom Sektore." *Menedzhment i Biznes-Administrirovaniye* 2: 162–85.

The Cranet Survey: Improving on a Challenged Research-Practice?

Jesper Christensen, Frans Bévort and Erling Rasmussen

Abstract: The Cranet-survey has mapped human resource management (HRM) practices for more than 25 years, and so it is timely to take a closer look at the significance of this unique multinational, longitudinal, empirical endeavor. How may we understand the inner workings and emergent practices of this ambitious research effort in order to better assess the value of the unique data-set and propose avenues for its improvement? This is of course a daunting task if the purpose is to make a general evaluation, as was the case in 2011 in the *Human Resource Management Review* issue on the Cranet International Network. Rather, the contribution of this article is to examine the established research practices of the Cranet Network from the point of view of incoming researchers to identify and assess fundamental challenges of design, measurement, and project management that underlie many of the more apparent and often-discussed issues relating to validity, comparability, and the multinational adaptation of standardized research tools. To accomplish this, the article analyzes the Danish Cranet project from its inception in 1991 until today, with particular emphasis on the effort to establish a longitudinally comprehensive Danish database with application in cross-country comparisons, exemplified here through comparisons with New Zealand. On this basis, the article discusses the ramifications for the Cranet Network and proposes opportunities and potentials for improving future consistency and comparability of the global research practice.

INTRODUCTION

When you approach the Cranet-project, as a new researcher, you cannot help being in awe of the sheer size of the venture both in terms of topical, geographical, and temporal scope. It is indeed unique, as emphasized by many comparative human resource management (HRM) researchers (e.g., Brewster, Mayrhofer, and Reichel 2011; Steinmetz et al. 2011). However, there are also concerns regarding the relative validity and comparability of such standardized surveys. How much valuable information is actually filtering through all these standardizing procedures, translations, and contextually colored interpretations?

Despite these caveats, the data Cranet provides are probably the best source if we want to state something general about how HRM practitioners evaluate HRM practices over time. We honestly recognize the value of a gargantuan effort like the Cranet Project, and a way to do this is to demonstrate how the data can be used. We use the comparison of the professionalization of HR in Denmark and New Zealand as an example here. As shown, New Zealand is a nation of comparable size and industrial structure (e.g., strong farming tradition, late industrialization), and the Cranet-survey is able to provide us comprehensive information on how the HR-profession in the two countries has evolved comparatively. And it can, indeed. In the short analysis, we show how the data can support several interesting hypotheses about the professionalization of HRM. However, what happens to our evaluation of the results if we look into the *black box of research practice* of a project like Cranet, as we will do in the following sections of the article?

When we discuss "research practice" instead of, for instance, "methodology," it is because we accept that what is at issue here is not merely a question about choosing to apply a specific methodology, be it more or less rigorous. "Research practice" is what, through the passing of time, grows out of a complex scientific venture like the Cranet project, as a result of multiple actions taken by multiple actors, inevitably resulting in intended as well as unintended effects. We are not cherishing naïve hopes that this complex organization can be reformed to some sort of fully transparent, orderly, and neat operation. At the same time, we think that it is possible to identify and address some of the variation which stems from this research practice, and develop it in a productive way by recognizing its nature openly.

Therefore, we outline the general methodology discussions of comparative longitudinal surveys, such as the Cranet-survey. The different concerns of adaptation and standardization are presented to give a general framework with which to discuss the examples of the Cranet-research practice and the paradoxical consequences of measuring differentiation by standardizing the measuring method.

We then analyze examples of the Cranet research practice based on reflections, on an established research practice by new Cranet researchers, partly based on our administration of the Danish Cranet survey 2014, and partly on our effort to establish a systematized database. In the process, we exemplify the unintended consequences of research practice by showing how these affect an analysis as the Denmark–New Zealand comparison. Furthermore, we report the challenges encountered and our findings on the consequences of irregularities and unnoticed adjustments when we went deeper into the methodological machinery of the survey. For instance, after working with the data, we found that less than 60 percent of the questions remained consistent over two or more recurrent surveys.

Generally, the article aims to answer three questions. First, what characterizes the Cranet Survey as a research practice? Second, how does the data and research tool match our expectations of methodological rigor? And finally, how is it possible to address problems of variance arising from other sources than the data itself without resorting to either unproductive standardization or, on the other hand, complete national autonomy in the design of the survey? In order to answer this, we introduce and analyze the concepts of *variance identification* and *variance distribution* to provide an alternative and more implementable solution to the standardization-autonomy tradeoff.

PROFESSIONALIZATION OF HRM IN DENMARK AND NEW ZEALAND

In the following, we compare and interpret the differences in the historical development and professionalization of HRM in Denmark and New Zealand. After making the case for the comparison, we carry out the analysis of the data. The analysis provides a context for the following discussion of how data are affected by the unintended variance stemming from research practice, affecting the whole objective of longitudinal, comparability, which is critical to the Cranet-survey.

Denmark and New Zealand are in many ways similar: in population size, historical industrial development, openness of the economy, and educational aspirations. However, Table 1 also illustrates that there are important differences (Table 1 is based on OECD data (www. data.oecd.org) accessed on the 8 January 2016).

Although New Zealand and Denmark are almost antipodes, there are many conspicuous similarities. Historically, both countries have a strong agricultural sector and they have open economies with a high degree of trade with the rest of the world, which means they have been exposed to international competition. However, post-1980s changes have put the two countries on different paths, with New Zealand known for its free-market, deregulated approach, and Denmark for its extensive welfare state and high taxation regime (Rasmussen and Lind 2013). These differences can be detected in terms of internationalization of the economy, composition of exports (New Zealand is still reliant on primary sector exports),

TABLE 1
Comparing Fundamental Societal Data on New Zealand and Denmark

	New Zealand	*Denmark*
Population	4,500,000	5,600,000
Density (capita per km^2)*	17	133
GDP (per capita USD)	38,113	46,000
Exports (mil. USD 2014)	41,948	111,726
Exports (% of GDP)	29	53
Agriculture (% of exports)	45	19
Tax revenue (USD per capita)	14,676	31,054
Social spending (%)	20.8	30.1
Income inequality (Gini)	0.33	0.25
Employment rate (%)	74	74
Hours worked per worker	1763	1436
Unemployment (%)	5.8	6.6
Long-term unempl. (% of unemployed)	13.6	25.2
Self-employment rate (%)	15.3	9.0
Trade union memb. (% of employed) 2000	22	74
Trade union memb. (% of employed) 2013	19	67
Internet access (%)	80	92
Road accidents (per 1 million cap.)	65	34

*Wikipedia, New Zealand, Denmark, 08-02-2016.

TABLE 2
Existence of a HR Department

	Country/Year of Survey							
	NZ 1997	DK 1999	NZ 2004	DK 2003	NZ 2011	DK 2008	NZ 2015	DK 2014
Do you have an HR department?								
No	221	55	71	71	12	29	15	45
	39.3%	13.7%	24.7%	14.2%	8.5%	8.0%	18.8%	18.8%
Yes	342	626	220	428	129	333	65	193
	60.7%	85.3%	75.3%	85.8%	90.8%	92.0%	81.3%	81.1%

spending on social welfare, and taxation levels. They have also influenced differences in terms of economic wealth and income inequality. The labor market measures of annual working hours and trade union density are also markedly different.

Thus, changes to economic, social, and labor market policies over the last decades have overlaid previous similarities, and thus, one could argue in favor of both convergence and divergence of the HRM-practice in New Zealand and Denmark. Recently, Capelli (2015) has suggested that the relative criticism and praise of HRM are cyclically and institutionally determined and has pointed out how the role of labor market institutions also creates different levels of interest in and focus on HR. For instance, he argues that a lower interest in HRM in United States is because interests of US employers are unfettered by unionized labor and government regulation that could balance the interests in the labor market (Capelli 2015, 60). This is clearly also relevant in respect of New Zealand employers (see Foster et al. 2011; Rasmussen 2016) and in respect of Danish employers, where the opposite is the case.

The Cranet-data show that the presence of HR-department in organizations in New Zealand is catching up with Danish level in the period from 60.7 percent in 1997 to 81.3 percent in 2015, while Danish organizations have had a coverage level of between 80–90 percent during the entire period (see Table 2). It is interesting to see that before and after the global financial crisis, situations result in approximately 10 percent fewer organizations reporting having an HR-department in 2014/2015. This could look like a "shake-out" of HR during the crises in a number of organizations, but overall, there is a high coverage of HR-departments in both countries in the period.

In Table 3, we get an indication of the size of the investment organizations do in the HR-department and specialized HR-activities. Two interesting conclusions spring to mind; while the staffing level in New Zealand remains stable (7–9), it seems as if there has been a strong growth in Denmark (from 8 to 14), with a minor backslide in 2014. This indicates that even though organizations in New Zealand have had a growing adoption of HR-departments, they do it with a relatively minor investment in manpower. This may be an example of the institutional differences mentioned. As shown above in Table 1, union membership coverage in Denmark is far the most comprehensive, which gives--following the Capelli argument--companies a greater impetus to invest in HR. Another outstanding feature is the "feminization" of HRM, which seems to be strong in both countries. However, the strongest trend is seen in New Zealand (from almost $4\male/5\female$ to $1\male/9\female$), while the Danish trend is almost stable (from

TABLE 3
Total Number of People Employed in HR Department (Mean Value)

	Country/Year of Survey							
	NZ 1997	DK 1999	NZ 2004	DK 2003	NZ 2011	DK 2008	NZ 2015	DK 2014
Total number of people employed in HR department	7	8	7	10	6	18	9	14
Total number of male employees in HR department	4	2	2	4	1	6	1	4
Total number of female employees in HR department	5	5	5	8	5	12	8	11

TABLE 4
HR Representation on the Board or Equivalent Top Executive Team

	Country/Year of Survey							
	NZ 1997	DK 1999	NZ 2004	DK 2003	NZ 2011	DK 2008	NZ 2015	DK 2014
Does the person responsible for HR have a place on the board or equivalent top executive team?								
No	200	220	131	206	40	139	25	70
	21.5%	57.2%	59.8%	47.2%	29.0%	38.9%	31.3%	29.8%
Yes	143	243	88	230	98	218	54	165
	25.1%	52.5%	40.2%	52.8%	71%	61.1%	67.5%	70.2%

2♂/5♀ to 4♂/11♀). Overall, the data support the general conclusion that, in those organizations who had already established them, HR departments have avoided being scaled back during the global financial crises (Bévort et al. 2014).

Another prevalent discussion point within HRM literature is the extent to which the HR-executive has access to top-management team. As seen from Table 4, it seems again as if New Zealand converges (from a lower level) to the situation in Denmark. While Table 4 shows a rise from 52.5 percent in 1999 to 70.2 percent in 2014 in Denmark, the New Zealand figures jump from 25.1 percent to 67.5 percent. The impression is that New Zealand, concerning a number of parameters within HRM, is following the trend in Denmark with a time lag of 5–10 years.

In terms of analyzing the professionalization of HRM, one of the important indicators is from where the HR executive is hired. Is experience in the local or another HR department valued or not? Is there an effective labor market for HR-executives/-managers? In Table 5, the background of the person responsible for HR is analyzed by four different sources: internal HR, internal Non-HR, external HR, and external Non-HR. A trend towards professionalization would suggest a higher proportion of managers hired from external HR-departments, with internal HR-department as the second choice, as the identity of the profession is becoming stronger. This is based on the observation that, as HR departments have become more widespread and populated by specialists, the stronger the choice the recruiting organization will have and thus it is both more attractive and feasible to hire from external, as well as internal HR-departments. On the other hand, there has been a counter-trend in favor of hiring non-HR specialists, in order to secure the business focus of the HR department.

TABLE 5
Recruitment of Person Responsible for HRM

	Country/Year of Survey							
	NZ 1997	DK 1999	NZ 2004	DK 2003	NZ 2011	DK 2008	NZ 2015	DK 2014
From where was the person responsible for HR recruited?								
From within the personnel/ HR department	55 10.7%	87 18.3%	22 8.1%	60 14.0%	22 16.1%	48 13.4%	16 21.3%	32 13.9%
From non-personnel/HR specialists in your organization	166 32.3%	179 37.6%	68 25.1%	164 38.2%	19 13.9%	89 24.9%	14 18.7%	72 31.2%
From personnel/HR specialists outside of the organization	190 37%	136 28.9%	125 46.1%	137 31.9%	79 57.7%	176 49.3%	37 49.3%	97 42.0%
From non-personnel/HR specialists outside of the organization	76 14.8%	74 15.5%	36 13.3%	68 15.9%	17 12.4%	44 12.3%	8 10.7%	30 13.0%

In New Zealand the proportion of HR-managers hired from own HR department has doubled from 1997 to 2015—from 10.7 percent to 21.9 percent—while the equivalent numbers are 18.3 percent to 13.9 percent in Denmark (in 1999 and 2014). When speaking of hiring from external HR departments, in New Zealand 37 percent of HR executives came from that source in 1997, while in Denmark the percentage was 28.9 percent in 1999. In 2015, the proportion in New Zealand was 49.3 percent versus 42 percent in Denmark. This indicates a relatively stronger trend towards a professional labor market for HR managers in New Zealand than in Denmark. In Denmark, it is generally more likely that the person responsible for HR is hired from outside the professional HR specialists.

Another strong indicator of professionalization is the seniority of the HR manager within the HR profession at the point of inquiry (Table 6). It is quite remarkable that the HR seniority of the HR managers is rising considerably in both countries over the periods we examine. To illustrate, we can use how the proportion of HR managers with more than 10 years of HR experience: In New Zealand in 1994 it was 34.9 percent, but in 2015 it was 45.3 percent. In Denmark, it was 25.5 percent in 1999, and 63.4 percent in 2014. The growing proportion indicates that HR careers are becoming more formalized and that many HR specialists stay within the profession when they advance. The numbers also point to a difference between New Zealand and Denmark, where the HR responsible person tends to have more HR professional seniority in Denmark, which goes along with the earlier observation of New Zealand being in a "runner up" position in terms of professionalization compared to Denmark.

Yet another indicator of professionalization is the level of academic training the HR managers have and the development towards a more sophisticated academic background (Table 7). The numbers show a very parallel development with 52.5 percent holding a university degree in New Zealand in 1994, and 56.5 percent in Denmark in 1999, and then rising to 75 percent (NZ, 2015) and 66.1 percent (DK, 2014), respectively. The numbers are not altogether unambiguous, but the general trend is from around 50 percent to around 70 percent with a university degree in the period. Here New Zealand seems to be a bit in front in terms of professionalization.

TABLE 6
Length of Service in HRM

| | Country/Year of Survey | | | | | | | |
	NZ 1997	DK 1999	NZ 2004	DK 2003	NZ 2011	DK 2008	NZ 2015	DK 2014
If working in HR, for how long? (intervals)								
<1 year	0	3	0	0	0	3	0	0
	0%	1.3%	0%	0%	0%	2.0%	0%	0%
1–2 years	12	79	23	31	5	14	10	8
	4.9%	33.5%	12.9%	10.3%	4.6%	9.2%	15.6%	6.1%
3–5 years	64	63	25	58	17	23	8	18
	26.2%	26.7%	14.0%	19.2%	15.6%	15.1%	12.5%	13.7%
6–9 years	83	31	27	68	14	20	17	22
	34.0%	13.1%	14.9%	22.5%	12.8%	13.2%	26.6%	16.8%
10–15 years	68	41	53	79	36	56	13	38
	27.9%	17.4%	29.8%	26.2%	33.0%	36.8%	20.3%	29.0%
>16 years	17	19	50	66	37	36	16	45
	7.0%	8.1%	28.1%	21.9%	33.9%	23.7%	25.0%	34.4%

TABLE 7
Education Level of HR Professional

| | Country/Year of Survey | | | | | | | |
	NZ 1997	DK 1999	NZ 2004	DK 2003	NZ 2011	DK 2008	NZ 2015	DK 2014
Do you have a university degree?								
No	260	222	95	221	35	88	20	59
	45.6%	43.5%	34.3%	43.7%	25.7%	26.8%	25%	33.9%
Yes	299	288	182	285	101	240	60	115
	52.5%	56.5%	65.7%	56.3%	74.3%	73.2%	75.0%	66.1%

On the surface, this is a very typical and intuitive way of using the Cranet data. We have a set of parameters, which are discussed along the longitudinal perspective and across two nations selected for their apparent similarities. We do think the analyses appear to make a lot of sense. They indicate how the development of HRM practices converges (in this case the relative professionalization of HR), even in countries situated as antipodes on the globe, albeit with a time lag in the case of New Zealand. The data also seems to lend credence to the institutional hypothesis promoted by Capelli (2015) and many others, that the social institutional context explains a lot of the relative prominence of HR in a specific country (with the difference in unionization between New Zealand and Denmark being very substantial). But our confidence in these interpretations and conclusions changes when we take into account some of what we know about the data collection and generation—and the choices made in that respect.

In the following, therefore, we investigate the influence of the actual research practice of the Cranet Survey on data and interpretations, such as those discussed above. Specifically, we discuss the general problems of comparability in multi-site longitudinal studies, and unpack the black box of the realized research practice and its consequences. The ultimate aim is to identify sources of unwanted variation and find ways to mitigate them to improve confidence in Cranet results and data.

REVISITING THE COMPARABILITY OBJECTIVE

Since its inception, the Cranet Survey has been international in outlook and comparative in purpose (Brewster, Hegewisch, and Lockhart 1991; Brewster et al. 1994). The intention to "[chart] the landscape of human resource management in different socio-cultural contexts and diverse geographical territories" is reflective of a pervasive trend towards comparative international research on management practices and strategy (Budhwar and Sparrow 2002; Brewster and Tyson 1991; Parry, Stavrou-Costea, and Morley 2011). In light of this, Morley (2007) distinguishes *three primary trajectories in contemporary HRM research*, each encompassing complementary aspects of the internationalization of HRM. One trajectory comprises studies on the role, use, and composition of HRM practices in multinational corporations and in the internationalization of firms in general (e.g., Brewster and Suutari 2005; Brewster, Wood, and Brookes 2008; Smale 2008). A second trajectory employs a more comparative lens to the study of HRM by emphasizing the impact of institutional, economic, and developmental differences on the country-specific adoption and adaptation of HR practices (e.g., Brewster, Larsen, and Trompenaars 1992; Croucher, Gooderham, and Parry 2006; Fenton-O'Creevy, Gooderham, and Nordhaug 2008). A third trajectory identifies national culture as a prime determinant of idiosyncrasies and similarities in HRM across national and cultural boundaries (e.g., Easterby-Smith, Malina, and Yuan 1995; Stavrou and Kilaniotis 2010; Vaiman and Brewster 2015). Despite their differences, these trajectories indicate a common ambition to identify and trace the evolution of HRM and HR practices within and across countries, institutions, and time. Indeed, many studies emerging from the Cranet Survey are not confined to a single trajectory, but rather seek to bridge several perspectives in order to account for and explain the complex interplay of contexts, cultures, and organizational practices (e.g., Brookes, Croucher, Fenton-O'Creevy, and Gooderham 2011; Papalexandris and Panayotopoulou 2004).

Notwithstanding the trajectories above, any ambition to do comparative and longitudinal research across countries must acknowledge an inherent dilemma (Brewster, Hegewisch, and Lockhart 1991, 37; Brewster and Tyson 1991, 8). On the one hand, the comparability and validity of cross-national findings rest on the similarity of measurement constructs, and the type of information collected. On the other hand, countries and the national features of HRM differ widely in institutional, economic, and cultural respects (Boon et al. 2009; Mayrhofer and Brewster 2005). Any attempt to standardize data collection will invariably reduce the ability to account for the impact of such idiosyncrasies. As discussed by Lazarova, Morley, and Tyson (2008, 1997), these necessary considerations have given rise to several debates within the HRM and Cranet community about the scope and conceptual delineations of HRM. For instance, the paradigmatic debate on universalist and contextual perspectives in HRM research and debates on national, cultural, and continental differences in HRM have fueled ongoing discussions, especially regarding the evidence for convergence or divergence of practices across countries (Brewster et al. 2007; Gooderham and Brewster 2008; Brewster, Mayrhofer, and Morley 2000; Brewster, Mayrhofer, and Reichel 2011).

Overall, scholars face a tradeoff in comparative HRM research between uncovering and accounting for national differences (a central objective of the Cranet Survey) and ensuring valid and meaningful comparability across countries. In the literature, methodological recommendations have clustered around two strategies for resolving or circumventing the tension: either greater standardization of procedures and constructs or greater survey adaptation to national contexts. Indeed, both strategies can be inferred from the prevalent ambition of Cranet scholars "to transcend the cultural differences of the researchers and converge to a standardized procedure of how the study has to be conducted . . . [by applying] a common research design . . . [consisting of] equivalent measures, that is, measures that are understood by respondents from different countries in the same way" (Steinmetz et al. 2011, 17).

The Cranet Survey reflects these considerations by promoting the adoption of a common research design across countries to foster greater comparability. Thus, each country is expected to adhere to common guidelines in implementation, including the use of a single respondent strategy (Gerhart 1999; Gerhart, Wright, and McMahon 2000), and a shared and standardized questionnaire that conforms to the ideal of equivalency in constructs and measurement (Hui and Triandis 1985; Steinmetz et al. 2011). Translation/back-translation is one of the most well-known methods used in pursuit of common measurements (Brislin 1970). At the same time, however, recommendations within the Cranet network acknowledge the need to allow for and encourage change and adaptation. At a global level, scholars convene periodically to assess and add to the existing set of questions and themes in order to accommodate trends and novel developments in HRM and in organizations at large (Lazarova, Morley, and Tyson 2008). At a local level, the research team is responsible for ensuring fit between the standardized questionnaire and the national context—specifically making sure that questions are understood, following translation/back-translation, while remaining true to the original intentions. Similarly, the local team has significant autonomy and, hence, responsibility in constructing and maintaining a relevant sampling frame (Häder and Gabler 2003; Tregaskis et al. 2004), including the crucial balancing act between source triangulation and constraints imposed by resources or institutions.

We propose that this inherent tradeoff between standardization and adaptation strategies is affected by idiosyncrasies in the concrete research practices performed in each country. In order to be able to make deliberate research strategies that take this tradeoff into account, we need therefore to explore and understand the impact of local variations, and attempt to identify systematic and predictable patterns in how these variations impact research outcomes.

INSIGHTS FROM THE DANISH CRANET SURVEYS

Given the *raison d'être* of the Cranet Survey to generate nationally and temporally comparable HRM data, the schism between adaptation and standardization hints at a range of procedural and definitional challenges that may detract significantly from the validity, comparability, and overall usefulness of the results of the Cranet Survey. Specifically, we explore the development and execution of the Danish Cranet Survey and identify three core issues of design, measurement, and project management that permeate and dictate the quality of the outcomes in the Danish research team over a 25-year period. We show how insufficient attention to particular elements within these categories, e.g., knowledge retention, sample development, database continuity, institutional impact, and definitional creep, seem to render the higher-level debates on adaptation or standardization moot, as the longitudinal and comparative qualities of the data hinge, at least in part, on a much more basic set of challenges.

Our discussion of these base level elements demonstrates that the relevant decision for Cranet researchers is not in choosing either standardization or country-specific adaptation as their sole strategy. Nor is it feasible to attempt to dissolve the tradeoff by imposing singular policies across national research teams, or by allocating significant additional resources to expanding the scope of the survey instrument or the number of researchers involved. Rather, the most effective solution to long-term validity lies in proper identification and management of the variations in data that are inevitably produced over time and between countries.

In turn, we argue that communicating and addressing these issues across participant countries is crucial to support the maturation of the Cranet Survey as a research practice in pursuit of its objectives. Building on and providing evidence of the conceptual concerns raised in previous contributions (e.g. Brewster, Mayrhofer, and Reichel 2011; Steinmetz et al. 2011), we contend that a more structured discussion of the identified base elements holds a key to balancing the opposing concerns of standardization and adaptation.

MANAGING LARGE-SCALE LONGITUDINAL RESEARCH EFFORTS

When any research practice is conducted and maintained across time and space, it becomes a central challenge to organize and manage the interactions among members and their adherence to principles and practices of the organization (Easterby-Smith and Malina 1999; Geringer, Frayne, and Milliman 2002; Mayrhofer 1998), even when organizing is achieved by virtual (Chesbrough and Teece 1996) or temporary means (Lundin and Söderholm 1995). Indeed, "managing international research networks over an extended period of time is important for achieving specific kinds of results, in particular country-comparative longitudinal analyses. Yet, the problems linked with it are only rarely addressed in the management literature" (Brewster, Mayrhofer, and Reichel 2011, 5). One such problem relates to responsibility and the maintenance of procedural insights over time.

At the very foundations of international research networks such as the Cranet Project lies the assumption that knowledge of existing procedures for collecting, structuring, and interpreting data are effectively shared and retained over time within each research unit (the national team) and, indeed, across the international organization in general. Longitudinal comparability within a single country, let alone across countries, hinges on the fact that members of the research team are able to effectively share and collectively adhere to similar procedures in data collection and data handling.

While seemingly a basic condition, this cannot be taken for granted. For instance, despite the Danish team being directed by the same senior manager during 1991–2008, the core research team underwent multiple changes in staffing, along with ongoing changes in the distribution of tasks and the involvement of external partners. The main reasons for these changes were staff availability and interest, as team members either became involved in more demanding research tasks elsewhere or developed their academic focus in other directions. At the same time, the Cranet head office experienced similar changes.

In concert, these changes produced a situation where "knowledge walks out the door" (Beazley, Boenisch, and Harden 2002:4; Parise, Cross, and Davenport 2006), which emphasizes the importance of managing knowledge retention in a research team, let alone in an international research network (e.g., Madsen, Mosakowski, and Zaheer 2002; 2003). In essence, vital information was not readily available to newcomers in the Danish team. It was exceedingly difficult to retrieve any information as to how the core population of organizations had been determined and how representative samples had been drawn in previous rounds of the survey apart from patchy and ultimately inadequate descriptions of methodology in country reports and associated publications. Relevant documentation and information had vanished with those responsible for the relevant tasks over the years and most of the actual sampling, data collection, and consolidation were undertaken by nonscientific partners with agendas of their own. The changing of the guard in the Cranet head office compounded these issues by making it more difficult to probe the international organization for information and documentation.

Importantly, the lack of information and relevant insights did not occur over night in the Danish case. Nor is it traceable to one particular instance of neglect or mismanagement. Rather the described situation emerged from a series of gradually accumulating events and decisions that would have seemed reasonable at the time (for example, the inclusion and reliance on nonscientific partners for particular subtasks). Yet, these seemingly minor decisions paved the way for significant challenges in terms of knowledge retention and consistent research practice. As knowledge walked out the door, the seeds were sown for other significant challenges to the consolidation, comparability, and validity of data.

Indeed, as the following sections illustrate, this absence of transparency with respect to both the changes made and the motivations for change has the effect of generating invisible variation across time periods and across countries that is exceedingly difficult for other researchers to identify, reproduce, and account for in later rounds of the survey. Additionally, and with more pernicious effects, the lack of continuity and transparency reduces the ability to gauge the consequences of incremental changes in measurements and sample construction, such as when research teams implement changes to the survey instrument to better reflect new trends or better capture certain phenomena through new measurement scales. When teams are ill-equipped to understand how elements of the survey tie together, and how they are used differently to either map longitudinal developments, make cross-national comparisons, or simply explore particular phenomena at a single point in time, the team is unlikely to appreciate how seemingly minor changes in phrasing or scaling can reduce the comparability and usefulness of the data for other researchers due to incongruent phrasing or irreconcilable scales.

Based on these observations, we propose that the management of longitudinal research projects, such as the Cranet Network, should emphasize the dual processes of variance identification and variance distribution. *Variance identification* addresses the issue of invisible variation over time and involves conscious efforts to elucidate and document changes made, as well as clear policies on how to mitigate the effects of unavoidable discontinuities in the research team. This is an effort to create greater transparency and take a more appreciative stance towards inevitable practice based variation, rather than ignoring it or trying to root it out completely. *Variance distribution* has to do with the unavoidable survey variation between countries and time periods that stems from shifting sampling conditions and changes in measurement. By identifying how individual survey items are different in terms of the objectives to which they mainly contribute[1], it is possible to describe interdependencies between different clusters of survey items.

This mapping provides a decision framework for research teams to better understand the compounding effects of changing one or more items, and to more easily identify ways of distributing the effects of the proposed change by adapting other items in the relevant cluster. In other words, the notion is to exploit overlaps between items to build in a higher level of active robustness and redundancy of information in the survey so as to retain sensitivity to local variation without compromising its general comparability. Both processes are expanded upon in the following sections.

DESIGN CHOICES AND INVISIBLE VARIATION: THE CASE OF BLACK BOX SAMPLING

Longitudinal survey designs offer a set of distinct advantages over cross-sectional research designs (Tourangeau 2003). Perhaps the most apparent advantage lies in the ability to identify and estimate within-subject change over time in response to changing conditions or, simply, due to the passage of time (Avey, Luthans, and Mhatre 2008). Furthermore, by allowing researchers to model time trends independently of other regressors (Wright 2007), the longitudinal design enables the comparison of within-subject and between-subject changes in the population over time. Such comparisons allow researchers to better determine the extent to which developments in the population are driven by clear changes among few members of the sample, or by more moderate changes across larger shares of the population).

To achieve the benefits of longitudinal designs, research teams have to ensure continuity of measurement and consistently representative samples. The importance of proper sample selection for the validity and comparability of survey results is well established in the literature on cross-cultural survey design (Häder and Gabler 2003; Nasif et al. 1991; Schaffer and Riordan 2003) and within Cranet methodology (Brewster, Mayrhofer, and Morley 2000; Steinmetz et al. 2011). In order to establish and validly test the statistical significance of any proposition, a representative sample must be drawn from the relevant population with a sufficient size to warrant statistical confidence (Fowler 2013). Barring situations where the entire population can be observed, statistical theory holds that a probability sampling strategy should be pursued in order to confer an equal likelihood of selection of all population members to minimize sampling and non-sampling errors, including non-response bias. However, in the Cranet Survey, as in most other empirical endeavors, practical realities, and constraints faced by researchers often lead to "far from ideal standards due to restrictions in time, money or human resources [in which case] applied research has to rely on convenience samples which represent the intended population to an unknown degree" (Steinmetz et al. 2011, 18).

While convenience and non-probability sampling is generally prominent (Bryman 2003, 113; Denscombe 2014, 49), it would seem particularly likely in the context of the Cranet Survey considering the difficulties associated with maintaining a sufficiently representative sampling frame of all large organizations, let alone an overview of the full population. Moreover, it has been observed that relevant databases of active organizations are often incomplete (Steinmetz et al. 2011). Consequently, the responsibility for selecting among available databases and including other relevant sources to approximate the true population befalls the country representatives (Tregaskis et al. 2004). This raises issues of generalizability, sampling error, non-response bias, and attrition (Lillard and Panis 1998; Hill and Willis 2001) that will be addressed differently and accounted for to varying degrees in different countries.

In Denmark, the 2014 Survey faced similar challenges. Echoing the lack of knowledge retention and transparent documentation of prior sampling strategies, there were no available records of the company population or associated contact information used in prior rounds. Moreover, it proved impossible to decipher which sampling frame had been used in prior rounds of the survey, let alone the sources used to establish the relevant population, because this information had not been spelled out in sufficient detail in prior publications. As such, the team had to decide, as a first step, whether to survey all companies in the population or to aim for a stratified sample. Given the relatively small size of the population in Denmark, it was deemed relevant to survey the entire sampling frame. Secondly, a sampling frame had to be constructed from available databases and supplemental sources. Sample construction began with the Danish Navne og Numre Erhverv (Names and Numbers Business, NNE) Database[2], which maintains an overview of key figures, ownership structure, industry, and other relevant information for all public and value added tax (VAT) registered companies in Denmark. The database contained information on approximately 2,200 unique companies and institutions (i.e., excluding subsidiaries and branches) in active operation with more than 100 employees (matching Cranet criteria). Preliminary sorting returned 2,160 relevant companies.

This presented another methodological challenge, however, as the degree to which this sample corresponded to the true population could not be sufficiently ascertained from this source alone. It is important to note that it would have been reasonable to base the survey on the sample, as the database in question was maintained by a dedicated company information provider with the explicit purpose of providing comprehensive data on the population. Hence, the retrieved data would presumably have represented a significant share of the underlying population. Nevertheless, the degree of representation and selection bias remained essentially unknown (cf. Steinmetz et al. 2011), and the team decided to exploit the fact that many complementary sources exist in Denmark. The retrieved list of companies was, therefore, triangulated with a similar query in the Experian Database, a global business information provider, as well as comparisons with membership information from Copenhagen Business School (CBS) Executive, an educational institution aimed at senior executives; the Network of Corporate Academies (NOCA), a membership organization focused on bridging research and practice in HRM; and DANSK HR, a network-based HR organization for executives and specialists with HRM responsibilities. Triangulation confirmed significant parts of the original list, while other parts were dropped or added, resulting in an ultimate sample of 2,118 companies. In order to counter possible response rate issues and reduce non-response bias, a significant amount of resources had to be invested in finding direct and updated contact information on the director and/or HR responsible individuals in each of the companies in the sample.

Despite our efforts to make our sampling frame as comprehensive as possible to ensure correspondence with prior sampling frames, we were unable to assess the degree to which our actual sample of respondent firms matched prior samples. Although summary statistics from past reports enabled comparisons in terms of industry compositions, firm size, formalization of HR practices, and similar aspects, we soon found several discrepancies that were not visible through summary statistics. In the Danish 2008 Cranet survey, for instance, the target population and sampling frame had apparently become mixed up with organization with less than 100 employees, which resulted in a much larger sampling frame compared to the one that was meticulously established in 2014. This effectively prevented us from assessing the comparative qualities of the actual samples, and due to the invisible nature of this variation, we were unable as well to control for these differences without significantly reducing the effective sample size or the number of available variables.

This issue of invisible variation through local adaptation is only compounded across borders. In the New Zealand 2011 Cranet report (Rasmussen and Ang 2013), the authors reflect upon changes to the sampling criteria, as the 1997 and 2004 Cranet surveys in New Zealand included organizations with 50 or more employees. In the Cranet format, small countries are allowed to sample below 100 employees so as to generate sufficient responses. However, it was decided in the subsequent surveys, in 2011 and 2015, to use 100 or more employees as the sampling criteria. This decision resides solely with the research team, but the decision of the original New Zealand team to use this threshold has impacted the comparability and validity of the data. For instance, in light of the received wisdom that HR formalization depends on firm size with the threshold for employing a fulltime HR-specialist being around 100 employees, the apparent delay in HR professionalization in New Zealand illustrated in the introduction would be attributable, in part, to the choice to expand the sampling frame with smaller organizations in 1997 and 2004. Additionally, the surveys were administered with time lags of up to three years between the two countries. In relation to the global financial crisis, for instance, this makes a substantial difference, since until 2008 most OECD countries were still growing strongly.

In 2011, the crisis had become evident and consequential in most countries, which is apparent in the Danish 2008 survey. In the four years described in the introduction, the Danish data indicate two opposing trends: a rise in the number of respondents holding a university degree from 2003 to 2008 and an equivalent fall from 2008 to 2014. This may indicate the influence of the crisis on the professionalization of HR in the two countries (though definite conclusions cannot be obtained before more rounds of the survey have been completed).

Controlling for such alternative cross-national explanations is a tremendous challenge and would reduce effective sample sizes and the number of available variables significantly. Thus, these invisible discrepancies demonstrate the importance of continuous documentation of design decisions, however benign or harmless they may seem in the short run. Specifically, it is necessary for research teams to communicate any deviations from the expected Cranet template on all matters of methodology, be it sampling frame, sample composition, methods of contacting respondent firms, adjustments to national or local limitations (e.g., few large organizations), or post-survey screening of responses, even when these activities have limited value for the present survey. This implies a need for formal support and recognition of the importance of such auxiliary activities to reduce the natural emphasis on the current survey and analyses.

MEASUREMENT ERROR AND VARIANCE DISTRIBUTION

While longitudinal surveys enable analyses of more expansive effects and an improved mapping of causal relationships compared to cross-sectional designs, they also introduce an additional set of potential measurement errors that need to be accounted for (Das, Toepoel, and van Soest 2011). The most prominent amongst these is sample attrition (Olson and Witt 2011; Zabel 1998), which denotes the tendency for respondents to drop from the sample in subsequent survey rounds. This has obvious implications for the ability to trace changes in time, but it also introduces significant bias, as attrition is rarely entirely random (Behr, Bellgardt, and Rendtel 2005; Olson and Witt 2011). Rather, attrition depends on respondent characteristics and inclinations (e.g., political/organizational interest correlates with likelihood of completing subsequent surveys), meaning that those who do not attrite are unlikely to be representative of the population (Bartels, 1999; Burden, 2000). And while it is possible to employ statistical imputation or post-stratification weights to partially account for the bias (Henderson, Hillygus, and Tompson 2010; Kalton and Kasprzyk 1986), these approaches tend to assume that respondents are missing at random and risk introducing significant bias if this assumption does not hold (Molenberghs et al. 2008).

Other important sources of measurement error in longitudinal research include conditioning effects and seam effects. Conditioning effects refer to the fundamental problem where participation in the survey impacts and conditions responses in subsequent rounds (Lazarsfeld 1940), either by affecting the motivation and awareness of respondents toward the topic, or by increasing respondent familiarity with the survey instrument (e.g., Kruse et al. 2009). Seam effects refer to the peculiar phenomenon where respondents tend to underestimate change when asked to compare multiple time periods in retrospect, but to overestimate changes when asked at different times (Conrad, Rips, and Fricker 2009). Whereas the suggestion regarding conditioning effects is to avoid them entirely by proper sampling, as "once they occur the resulting data are irredeemably biased" (Warren and Halpern-Manners 2012, 522), seam effects may be addressed within the survey by reversing question order or similarly promoting improved respondent reflection and recall (Rips, Conrad, and Fricker 2003).

What is common to these sources of measurement error is their dependence on respondents. Attrition effects, conditioning effects, and seam effects are all determined, in part, by the motivations and autonomous choices of respondents, which puts the effects outside the complete control of researchers. Another source of measurement error that is entirely under the control of researchers, and is therefore perhaps of more relevance to the present discussion, is the composition and design of survey items and associated measurement scales. When these undergo changes, even to relatively minor degrees, the comparison of data across time periods and countries may be compromised if questions are discontinued or merged, or if the scaling of questions leads them to become irreconcilable with prior measurements.

To see this, the reader should recall that an explicit purpose for the Danish team was to integrate the results of the 2014 survey with the data from previous years to construct a database capable of supporting the Cranet objective of longitudinal and cross-national comparisons. In light of the above sections, the assumption that this would be a rather straightforward exercise was perhaps naïve. Nevertheless, having adopted the standardized Cranet questionnaire and associated database structure, it was expected that codified data from previous years could be immediately integrated with the present survey to form a longitudinal dataset. In addition, given the push to standardize the questionnaire and data structure throughout the Cranet organization (Lazarova, Morley, and Tyson 2008), the data were expected to be easily comparable across countries.

Reflecting the issue of knowledge retention, the first challenge was to simply retrieve the relevant questionnaires and data files. We did not anticipate the fact that some questionnaires were not available in electronic form, but were fortunate enough that they had been stored physically in old archives. Regarding the files, there was no local archive, and the team had no knowledge of whom to ask. It eventually became necessary to contact the central Cranet secretariat in the UK and ask to tap into the central archives. With a diligent secretariat and a bit of luck, it was possible to locate the relevant files in different locations and often in the possession of random members (which incidentally shows the strength of the global network). However, the received files revealed a more daunting problem, as the data had by no means been formatted and labeled consistently over the years. Thus, the second and main challenge in constructing the database was to manually sift through each question from each round of the survey to establish which questions were longitudinally consistent.

We found that inconsistency involved several dimensions. First, questions were not necessarily maintained over time, and many questions had been dropped, merged, or included as adaptations to changing trends or emerging fields of interest. Secondly, even if a question had been retained throughout all surveys, small changes had often crept in over the years, presumably to improve the wording of a particular question or as a by-product of the translation/back-translation process (Brewster, Mayrhofer, and Reichel 2011; Brislin 1970). Third, measurement scales changed over time to different degrees. This ranged from small changes in Likert scale intervals or in the wording of response categories to relatively major shifts in question framing and response categories (e.g., moving from a focus on the presence or absence of a particular phenomenon to asking about the extent of that phenomenon, often in response to particular HR practices becoming more commonplace).

While the exclusion and inclusion of questions has obvious consequences for the longitudinal scope of the survey, changes in the definitions and wording of questions and response categories represent an underlying definitional creep (Strauss 2001, 886) that proved equally pernicious. Thus, even miniscule changes to the structure or wording of a question can have significant consequences. For example, seemingly irrelevant changes in Likert scale percentage intervals often forced the team to reduce the surveyed information to simple dummy variables measuring the presence or absence of the phenomenon in question, because intervals could not be adequately merged or aggregated over time. Similarly, when questions had been changed from a simple yes/no-categorization to a focus on the extent of the given phenomenon (often motivated by a genuine academic interest in mapping the dimensions of the phenomenon), researchers were faced with a tradeoff between detail and longitudinal comparability, because comparability could only be maintained by reducing the level of detail to the lowest common denominator (i.e., yes/no).

In essence, the process demonstrated the pervasive and detrimental influence of carelessness in survey implementation, but it also demonstrated the required depth-of-knowledge that the responsible team must possess in order to consciously introduce changes in the survey process, however interesting or academically well-founded they may be. To illustrate the magnitude of this problem, only 57 questions were consistent, or could be made consistent through reduction, across two or more survey rounds (excluding questions that had only appeared in one year). In respect of the questions in the 2014 survey in Denmark, this amounts to an inconsistency share of more than 30 percent of the questions that were repeated in two or more survey rounds.

Similar to attrition effects, conditioning effects, and seam effects, the described problems of consistency and measurement add to the total variation across time periods and between countries. While some of this variation is an unwanted by-product of the behavior of respondents, significant parts of it result from well-founded and theoretically relevant changes to the survey instrument. Hence, simply limiting the national teams in terms of their autonomy to adapt and improve upon the instrument is not a feasible solution. Rather, what we observed in our process was that the items that become inconsistent tend to cluster, and that different clusters require different levels of variance distribution. In particular, items in the Cranet survey differ with respect to the post-survey questions they are intended to answer. Some are only intended to measure new phenomena of interest in the given period or provide background information to properly control for variation in the present data (e.g., firm characteristics). These measures are robust to adaptation, as they are either limited to one time period or primarily used as auxiliary measures.

On the contrary, items intended for cross-country comparisons in one period or within-country longitudinal comparisons are far less robust to adaptation and require attention to other measures within the same cluster. As such, we found that many measures in these clusters could be made consistent through combinations with other questions that measured related aspects and thus provided information to bridge the gaps made by prior adjustments.

By exploiting these related measures, it is possible to distribute variance, using other items to mitigate the detrimental effects of adjustments.

The degree of inconsistency was seen to be particularly severe in items that lend themselves to hybrid analyses with both cross-country and longitudinal elements. Here, even minor adjustments may bias the item on one or both of these dimensions, making it significantly harder to locate relevant information from other questions to attempt to distribute and mitigate variation. Thus, these items require significantly more attention and most likely simultaneous adaptation of related questions to help distribute the resulting variance and mitigate the potential consequences.

We propose that variance distribution is an effective solution to the paradoxical tradeoff between standardization and adaptation. While we were fortunate to locate several useful items to base this distribution on in our analyses, the effectiveness of this process would benefit greatly from a more structured approach in national research teams. This would involve a conscious and continuous mapping of the interdependencies between items and the emergent clusters and, thereby, provide a kind of scaffolding to enable easier identification of items suited for variance distribution and items that need to be changed in concert with planned adaptations to ensure the possibility of variance distribution in later periods.

DISCUSSION AND CONCLUSIONS

At first glance, the significance of the above considerations could be rejected simply as procedural errors that could and should be weeded out through professional and conscientious conduct (see Lazarova, Morley, and Tyson 2008, 2000). However, while much can undoubtedly be gained through greater adherence to protocol and better application of the survey instrument, significant parts of the variation in the Cranet survey do not result from carelessness, but rather from theoretically relevant change. We argue, therefore, that the usefulness of the Cranet survey may be significantly improved by learning how to accommodate such variance, rather than simply increasing the level of standardization.

We are facing continuous challenges of declining response rates, effects of changing technologies, and an inevitable temporality of the national research teams (Hillygus et al. 2006). As such, our case has highlighted the importance of taking precautions to avoid knowledge walking out the door (Beazley, Boenisch, and Harden 2002:4). Despite the ongoing digitalization of scholarly work and our embeddedness within a vast and active network, there is good reason to investigate and implement countermeasures to the inevitable seeping of knowledge.

Importantly, this is not a simple question of safeguarding relevant documents or procedural insights on how the sampling and survey are best conducted. Instead, it has to do with the relevance of establishing and maintaining adequate knowledge of the nature and emergent development of the survey instrument to assess the consequences and validity of local adaptations and decisions on implementation strategy. We contend that without this knowledge, adaptations and implementation in general risk becoming haphazard and detrimental to the longitudinal validity of survey results. Indeed, the relevance of this contention is reflected in the discussion of definitional creep and the associated consequences for the quality and com-parability of data. Building on this, the Danish survey demonstrates the effects of triangulat-ing several sources of population data on the quality of the sampling frame.

The problem of maintaining a multinational, longitudinal survey has demanded constant convening of Cranet scholars to access and adjust the existing questionnaire to accommodate new developments and trends. The perennial issue of low response rates has also demanded ongoing changes and has likely been in the minds of most national teams as they interpreted findings and issues (see Rasmussen and Ang 2013, 11). Still, there are other challenges, which have to be overcome in order to secure the credibility of the project in the future. We have shown how complex the organization of such a project is and how much attention to detail and leadership is required to maintain an acceptable data consistency and integrity. There is a huge amount of tacit or implicit knowledge and skill, which must be shared syn-chronically and diachronically within the organization. In the Danish case, we saw examples of incomplete sharing of knowledge about technical issues and a very patchy accumulation and communication of data and crucial questions between survey rounds. As a result, defini-tions crept and more than 30 percent of the questions became inconsistent and less useful for longitudinal analysis.

There have already been considerable theoretical contributions on related methodological challenges (Brewster, Mayrhofer, and Reichel 2011; Parry, Stavrou-Costea, and Morley 2011; Steinmetz et al. 2011). This article points to the micro-research practices in each coun-try as being critical for the quality of data collected, and as a potential resolution of the entrenched tradeoff between standardization and adaptation. This issue has not been dis-cussed systematically in the literature and provides clear avenues for progress within the Cranet Project. Indeed, we find that most Cranet member countries approach similar obstacles and struggle with finding the appropriate balance—something that may well be exacerbated by the steadily growing number of members of the Cranet project.

We can do a better job! As such, this article is partly dedicated to incoming new members or new teams to assist in improving the surveys of the future. Thus, as a complement to the proposed importance of considering and actively engaging in the processes of variance iden-tification and variance distribution, we want to reiterate three basic recommendations with regard to knowledge retention, sample construction, and definitional integrity. Concerning knowledge retention, research teams need to look beyond the survey at hand and their descriptions of current data structures and empirical findings. They need to invest time in describing the deliberations underlying key decisions and prioritizations made in terms of sampling, questionnaire translation and distribution, data consolidation, analysis, and inter-pretation. While it may seem superfluous to expend resources on documenting these issues, the challenges posed by longitudinal and cross-national analyses call for an improved ability to identify variance by being able to unravel the ongoing methodological deliberations and decisions in order to inform new decisions and explain apparent anomalies in the data and comparisons of results. Teams must acknowledge the path dependency of decisions and refrain from blind dependence on the intrapersonal ability to codify and share relevant pro-cedural learning, which is sufficient in one-off studies but dangerous in longitudinal projects. Moreover, the use of external partners should continue, as it enables greater quality in many instances, but should be accompanied by the awareness of the potential impact on knowledge retention of outsourcing tasks to nonscientific partners. Lastly, knowledge retention should be underpinned by a structured archive for questionnaires, data files, and other relevant material to support teams down the road.

Regarding *sample construction*, an important part of a tenable research practice is to thoroughly consider the benefits of engaging in triangulation. The objective of improving the sampling frame prior to undertaking the actual survey should be traded off against the costs of pursuing triangulation, as well as the institutional possibilities of doing so (e.g., the amount and quality of (public) databases and relevant institutional actors from whom to draw relevant company and contact information). It follows that a core element of research practice is the criteria used to assess the adequacy of the sampling frame at hand. As such, it may well be that satisfying is the most feasible strategy for a particular research team if investments in further triangulation are likely to only confirm the extant sample and provide little further value. However, it may be impossible for a research team to reach this conclusion in advance, without tapping into the experiences of prior research team members.

Finally, regarding *definitional integrity*, the key recommendation is to establish and maintain transparency in terms of labeling, formatting, and general data structure across survey rounds. When these criteria are not met, consolidation and analysis require a large effort in terms of reviewing, sorting, and ultimately reducing data from previous years because of uncertainty and inconsistency. In the words of thisarticle, variance distribution becomes significantly harder to accomplish. To avoid undermining the usefulness of the longitudinal data, research teams must be highly consistent in their terminology and avoid any unnecessary deviations in labeling and measurement. To accomplish this, a consistent and updated database should be maintained to provide a template for the construction and integration of new surveys. In situations when the predicted consequences of a proposed change (e.g., decreased comparability or reductions in sample size or measurement specificity) cannot be meaningfully distributed and mitigated through adaptations of related items, the value of the change must be assessed against this backdrop, rather than being assessed only on the theoretical merits of the change.

By becoming more reflexive and experienced in terms of research practice, teams are better positioned to conduct future surveys, as well as predict and assess the consequences of necessary adaptations in the local context. Hence, improving the research practices of teams in each participant country would likely enable a greater flexibility in adapting to and accounting for local variation without compromising the overarching ambition of cross-national and longitudinal comparability.

Notes

1. We distinguish four main objectives (see Table 1). These include comparisons across countries within one time period; longitudinal comparisons within one country; hybrid comparisons of time trends across countries; or simple tests of particular phenomena within one country in one time period.

2. Navne and Numre Erhverv, http://erhverv.nnmarkedsdata.dk/Content/Search/Common
   Search.aspx?focusnews=104

REFERENCES

Avey, J. B., F. Luthans, and K. H. Mhatre. 2008. "A Call for Longitudinal Research in Positive Organizational Behavior." *Journal of Organizational Behavior* 29 (5):705–11. doi:10.1002/job.517.

Bartels, L. M. 1999. "Panel Effects in the American National Election Studies." *Political Analysis* 8 (1):1–20. doi: 10.1093/oxfordjournals.pan.a029802.

Beazley, H., J. Boenisch, and D. Harden. 2002. *Continuity Management: Preserving Corporate Knowledge and Productivity When Employees Leave.* Hoboken, NJ: John Wiley and Sons.

Behr, A., E. Bellgardt, and U. Rendtel. 2005. "Extent and Determinants of Panel Attrition in the European Community Household Panel." *European Sociological Review* 21 (5):489–512. doi:10.1093/esr/jci037.

Bévort, F., H. H. Larsen, A. Hjalager, and J. Christensen. 2014. *HRM Efter Krisen. Back to Square One Eller Fugl Fønix.* Copenhagen, Denmark: Cranet Projektet/Academic Books.

Boon, C., J. Paauwe, P. Boselie, and D. Den Hartog. 2009. "Institutional Pressures and HRM: Developing Institutional Fit." *Personnel Review* 38 (5):492–508. doi:10.1108/00483480910978018.

Brewster, C., R. Croucher, G. Wood, and M. Brookes. 2007. "Collective and Individual Voice: Convergence in Europe?" *The International Journal of Human Resource Management* 18 (7):1246–62. doi:10.1080/09585190701393582.

Brewster, C., A. Hegewisch, and J. Lockhart. 1991. "Researching Human Resource Management: Methodology of the Price Waterhouse Cranfield Project on European Trends." *Personnel Review* 20 (6):36–40. doi:10.1108/EUM0000000000804.

Brewster, C., A. Hegewisch, L. Mayne, and O. Tregaskis. 1994. "Methodology of the Price Waterhouse Cranfield Project." In *Policy and Practice in European Human Resource Management*, edited by C. Brewster and A. Hegewisch. London, UK: Routledge.

Brewster, C., H. H. Larsen, and F. Trompenaars. 1992. "Human Resource Management in Europe: Evidence from Ten Countries." *International Journal of Human Resource Management* 3 (3):409–34.

Brewster, C., W. Mayrhofer, and M. Morley. 2000. *New Challenges for European Human Resource Management.* London, UK: Palgrave Macmillan.

Brewster, C., W. Mayrhofer, and A. Reichel. 2011. "Riding the Tiger? Going along with Cranet for Two Decades - A Relational Perspective." *Human Resource Management Review* 21 (1):5–15. doi:10.1016/j.hrmr.2010.09.007.

Brewster, C., and V. Suutari. 2005. "Global HRM: Aspects of a Research Agenda." *Personnel Review* 34 (1):5–21. doi:10.1108/00483480510571851.

Brewster, C., and S. Tyson. 1991. *International Comparisons in Human Resource Management.* London, UK: Financial Times Management.

Brewster, C., G. Wood, and M. Brookes. 2008. "Similarity, Isomorphism or Duality? Recent Survey Evidence on the Human Resource Management Policies of Multinational Corporations." *British Journal of Management* 19 (4):320–42. doi:10.1111/j.1467-8551.2007.00546.x.

Brislin, R. W. 1970. "Back-Translation for Cross-Cultural Research." *Journal of Cross-Cultural Psychology* 1 (3): 185–216. doi:10.1177/135910457000100301.

Brookes, M., R. Croucher, M. Fenton-O'Creevy, and P. Gooderham. 2011. "Measuring Competing Explanations of Human Resource Management Practices through the Cranet Survey: Cultural versus Institutional Explanations." *Human Resource Management Review* 21 (1):68–79. doi:10.1016/j.hrmr.2010.09.012.

Bryman, A. 2003. *Research Methods and Organization Studies.* London, UK: Routledge.

Budhwar, P. S., and P. R. Sparrow. 2002. "An Integrative Framework for Understanding Cross-National Human Resource Management Practices." *Human Resource Management Review* 12 (3):377–403. doi:10.1016/S1053-4822(02)00066-9.

Burden, B. C. 2000. "Voter Turnout and the National Election Studies." *Political Analysis* 8 (4):389–98. doi:10.1093/oxfordjournals.pan.a029823.

Capelli, P. 2015. "Why we Love to Hate HR ... and What HR Can Do about It." *Harvard Business Review* 93 (7–8):54–61.

Chesbrough, H. W., and D. J. Teece. 1996. "When Is Virtual Virtuous?" *Harvard Business Review* 74 (1):65–73.

Conrad, F. G., L. J. Rips, and S. S. Fricker. 2009. "Seam Effects in Quantitative Responses." *Journal of Official Statistics* 25 (3):1–24.

Croucher, R., P. Gooderham, and E. Parry. 2006. "The Influences on Direct Communication in British and Danish Firms: Country 'Strategic HRM' or Unionization?" *European Journal of Industrial Relations* 12 (3):267–86. doi: 10.1177/0959680106068913.

Das, M., V. Toepoel, and A. Van Soest. 2011. "Nonparametric Tests of Panel Conditioning and Attrition Bias in Panel Surveys." *Sociological Methods & Research* 40 (1):32–56. doi:10.1177/0049124110390765.

Denscombe, M. 2014. *The Good Research Guide: For Small-Scale Social Research Projects*. UK: McGraw-Hill Education.

Easterby-Smith, M., and D. Malina. 1999. "Cross-Cultural Collaborative Research: Toward Reflexivity." *Academy of Management Journal* 42 (1):76–86. doi:10.5465/256875.

Easterby-Smith, M., D. Malina, and L. Yuan. 1995. "How Culture-Sensitive Is HRM? A Comparative Analysis of Practice in Chinese and UK Companies." *The International Journal of Human Resource Management* 6 (1): 31–59. doi:10.1080/09585199500000002.

Fenton-O'Creevy, M., P. Gooderham, and O. Nordhaug. 2008. "Human Resource Management in US Subsidiaries in Europe and Australia: Centralization or Autonomy?" *Journal of International Business Studies* 39 (1):151–66. doi:10.1057/palgrave.jibs.8400313.

Foster, B., E. Rasmussen, I. Laird, and J. Murrie. 2011. "Supportive Legislation, Unsupportive Employers and Collective Bargaining in New Zealand." *Relations Industrielles* 66 (2):192–212. doi:10.7202/1006116ar.

Fowler, F. J. Jr, 2013. *Survey Research Methods*. London, UK: Sage Publications.

Gerhart, B. 1999. "Human Resource Management and Firm Performance: Measurement Issues and Their Effect on Causal and Policy Inferences." *Research in Personnel and Human Resources Management* 4 supplement :31–51.

Gerhart, B., P. M. Wright, G. C. McMahan, and S. A. Snell. 2000. "Measurement Error in Research on Human Resources and Firm Performance: How Much Error is There and How Does it Influence Effect Size Estimates?" *Personnel Psychology* 53 (4):803–34.

Geringer, J. M., C. A. Frayne, and J. F. Milliman. 2002. "In Search of 'Best Practices' in International Human Resource Management: Research Design and Methodology." *Human Resource Management* 41 (1):5–30. doi:10. 1002/hrm.10017.

Gooderham, P. N., and C. Brewster. 2008. "Convergence, Stasis or Divergence? The Case of Personnel Management in Europe." In *Current Issues in International Human Resource Management and Strategy Research*, edited by M. Festing and S. Rpyer, 141–56. München, Germany: Rainer Hampp Verlag.

Häder, S., and S. Gabler. 2003. "Sampling and Estimation." In *Cross Cultural Survey Methods*, edited by J. Harkness, F. Van De Vijver, and P. Mohler. New York, NY: Wiley.

Henderson, M., D. S. Hillygus, and T. Tompson. 2010. "Sour Grapes or Rational Voting? Voter Decision Making among Thwarted Primary Voters in 2008." *Public Opinion Quarterly* 74 (3):499–529. doi:10.1093/poq/nfq008.

Hill, D. H., and R. J. Willis. 2001. "Reducing Panel Attrition: A Search for Effective Policy Instruments." *The Journal of Human Resources* 36 (3):416–38. doi:10.2307/3069625.

Hillygus, D. S., N. H. Nie, K. Prewitt, and H. Pals. 2006. *The Hard Count: The Political and Social Challenges of Census Mobilization*. New York, NY: Russell Sage Foundation.

Hui, C. H., and H. C. Triandis. 1985. "Measurement in Cross-Cultural Psychology: A Review and Comparison of Strategies." *Journal of Cross-Cultural Psychology* 16 (2):131–52.

Kalton, G., and D. Kasprzyk. 1986. "The Treatment of Missing Survey Data." *Survey Methodology* 12 (1):1–16.

Kruse, Y., M. Callegaro, J. M. Dennis, S. Subias, M. Lawrence, C. Disogra, and T. Tompson. 2009. "Panel Conditioning and Attrition in the AP-Yahoo! News Election Panel Study." Paper presented at the 64th Conference of the American Association for Public Opinion Research (AAPOR), Hollywood, FL.

Lazarova, M., M. Morley, and S. Tyson. 2008. "International Comparative Studies in HRM and Performance–the Cranet Data: Introduction." *The International Journal of Human Resource Management* 19 (11):1995–2003. doi:10.1080/09585190802404239.

Lazarsfeld, P. F. 1940. "Panel Studies." *Public Opinion Quarterly* 4 (1):122–8. doi:10.1086/265373.

Lillard, L. A., and C. W. Panis. 1998. "Panel Attrition from the Panel Study of Income Dynamics: Household Income, Marital Status, and Mortality." *The Journal of Human Resources* 33 (2):437–57. doi:10.2307/ 146436.

Lundin, R. A., and A. Söderholm. 1995. "A Theory of the Temporary Organization." *Scandinavian Journal of Management* 11 (4):437–55. doi:10.1016/0956-5221(95)00036-U.

Madsen, T. L., E. Mosakowski, and S. Zaheer. 2002. "The Dynamics of Knowledge Flows: Human Capital Mobility, Knowledge Retention and Change." *Journal of Knowledge Management* 6 (2):164–76. doi:10.1108/13673270210424684.

Madsen, T. L., E. Mosakowski, and S. Zaheer. 2003. "Knowledge Retention and Personnel Mobility: The Non-Disruptive Effects of Inflows of Experience." *Organization Science* 14 (2):173–91. doi:10.1287/orsc.14.2.173.14997.

Mayrhofer, W. 1998. "Between Market, Bureaucracy and Clan: Coordination and Control Mechanisms in the Cranfield Network on European Human Resource Management (Cranet-E)." *Journal of Managerial Psychology* 13 (3/4):241–58. doi:10.1108/02683949810215057.

Mayrhofer, W., and C. Brewster. 2005. "European Human Resource Management: Researching Developments over Time." *Management Revu* 16 (1):36–62. doi:10.5771/0935-9915-2005-1-36.

Mayrhofer, W., C. C. Brewster, M. J. Morley, and J. Ledolter. 2011. "Hearing a Different Drummer? Convergence of Human Resource Management in Europe—a Longitudinal Analysis." *Human Resource Management Review* 21 (1):50–67. doi:10.1016/j.hrmr.2010.09.011.

Molenberghs, G., C. Beunckens, C. Sotto, and M. G. Kenward. 2008. "Every Missingness Not at Random Model Has a Missingness at Random Counterpart with Equal Fit." *Journal of the Royal Statistical Society: Series B (Statistical Methodology)* 70 (2):371–88. doi:10.1111/j.1467-9868.2007.00640.x.

Morley, M. 2007. "Of Infants and Adolescents: Progress and Pessimism in the Development Trajectory of International Human Resource Management". Keynote Presentation to the 9th IHRM Conference Estonia, Tallinn, June 12–15.

Nasif, E. G., H. Al-Daeaj, B. Ebrahimi, and M. S.Thibodeaux. 1991. "Methodological Problems in Cross-Cultural Research: An Updated Review." *Management International Review* 31 (1):79–91.

Olson, K., and L. Witt. 2011. "Are we Keeping the People Who Used to Stay? Changes in Correlates of Panel Survey Attrition over Time." *Social Science Research* 40 (4):1037–50. doi:10.1016/j.ssresearch.2011.03.001.

Papalexandris, N., and L. Panayotopoulou. 2004. "Exploring the Mutual Interaction of Societal Culture and Human Resource Management Practices: Evidence from 19 Countries." *Employee Relations* 26 (5):495–509. doi:10.1108/01425450410550473.

Parise, S., R. Cross, and T. H. Davenport. 2006. "Strategies for Preventing a Knowledge-Loss Crisis." *MIT Sloan Management Review* 47 (4):31–8.

Parry, E., E. Stavrou-Costea, and M. J. Morley. 2011. "The Cranet International Research Network on Human Resource Management in Retrospect and Prospect." *Human Resource Management Review* 21 (1):1–4. doi:10.1016/j.hrmr.2010.09.006.

Rasmussen, E. 2016. "A Comparative Perspective on Collective Bargaining and the Role of Employers." In *Den Danske Model Set Udefra*, edited by T.P. Larsen and A. Ilsøe. Copenhagen, Denmark: FAOS.

Rasmussen, E., and J. Lind. 2013. "In Support of a New Zealand 'Living Wage': Reflections on Danish 'Working Poor' Trends and Issues." *New Zealand Journal of Employment Relations* 38 (2):17–32.

Rasmussen, E., and A. Ang. 2013. "Cranet-Survey on International Strategic Human Resource Management: Report on the New Zealand Findings from the 2011–12 Survey." Department Of Management, Auckland University of Management.

Rips, L. J., F. G. Conrad, and S. S. Fricker. 2003. "Straightening the Seam Effect in Panel Surveys." *Public Opinion Quarterly* 67 (4):522–54. doi:10.1086/378962.

Schaffer, B. S., and C. M. Riordan. 2003. "A Review of Cross-Cultural Methodologies for Organizational Research: A Best-Practices Approach." *Organizational Research Methods* 6 (2):169–215. doi:10.1177/1094428103251542.

Smale, A. 2008. "Global HRM Integration: A Knowledge Transfer Perspective." *Personnel Review* 37 (2):145–64. doi:10.1108/00483480810850515.

Stavrou, E., and C. Kilaniotis. 2010. "Flexible Work and Turnover: An Empirical Investigation across Cultures." *British Journal of Management* 21 (2):541–54. doi:10.1111/j.1467-8551.2009.00659.x.

Steinmetz, H., C. Schwens, M. Wehner, and R. Kabst. 2011. "Conceptual and Methodological Issues in Comparative HRM Research: The Cranet Project as an Example." *Human Resource Management Review* 21 (1):16–26. doi:10.1016/j.hrmr.2010.09.008.

Strauss, G. 2001. "HRM in the USA: Correcting Some British Impressions." *The International Journal of Human Resource Management* 12 (6):873–97. doi:10.1080/09585190122941.

Tourangeau, R. 2003. "Recurring Surveys: Issues and Opportunities." Report to the National Science Foundation, March 28–29, National Science Foundation, Arlington, VA.

Tregaskis, O., C. Mahoney, S. Atterbury, C. Brewster, W. Mayrhofer, and M. J. Morley. 2004. "International Survey Methodology: Experiences from the Cranet Survey." In *Human Resource Management in Europe: Evidence of Convergence?* edited by C. Brewster, W. Mayrhofer and M.J. Morley, 437–50. Oxford, UK: Butterworth-Heinemann.

Vaiman, V., and C. Brewster. 2015. "How Far Do Cultural Differences Explain the Differences between Nations? Implications for HRM." *The International Journal of Human Resource Management* 26 (2):151–64. doi:10.1080/09585192.2014.937969.

Warren, J. R., and A. Halpern-Manners. 2012. "Panel Conditioning in Longitudinal Social Science Surveys." *Sociological Methods & Research* 41 (4):491–534. doi:10.1177/0049124112460374.

Wright, T. A. 2007. "A Look at two Methodological Challenges for Scholars Interested in Positive Organizational Behavior." In *Positive Organizational Behavior: Accentuating the Positive at Work*, edited by D. Nelson and C. L. Cooper, 177–90. Thousand Oaks, CA: Sage.

Zabel, J. E. 1998. "An Analysis of Attrition in the Panel Study of Income Dynamics and the Survey of Income and Program Participation with Application to a Model of Labor Market Behavior." *Journal of Human Resources* 33 (2):479–506. doi:10.2307/146438.

Index

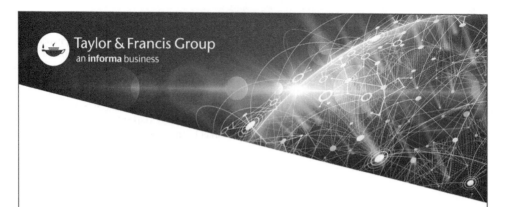